Presented to

_____

from

_____

UNDERSTANDING THE
66 BOOKS OF THE BIBLE

with Dr. David Jeremiah

Edited by Robert J. Morgan
Unless otherwise indicated, Scripture verses quoted are from the
NEW KING JAMES VERSION.

Printed in the United States of America.

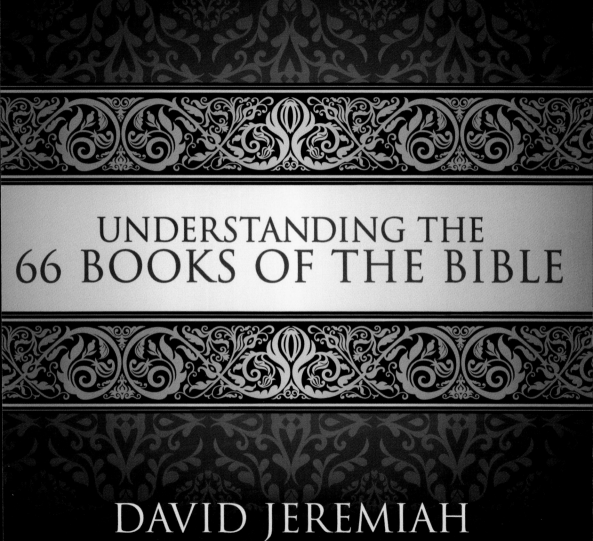

UNDERSTANDING THE
66 BOOKS OF THE BIBLE

DAVID JEREMIAH

Table of Contents

NEW TESTAMENT

Introduction

The Bible contains everything we need to know for time and eternity. It's the wisdom of God distilled for human consumption. It's the mind of Christ between two covers; knowledge that enlightens, advice that counsels, food that feeds, milk that nourishes, honey that sweetens, gold that enriches, a sword that defends, a hammer that molds us, and a lamp that guides us.

Every word of the Bible was penned by a person like you or me, yet each word was breathed out by God as holy men of old spoke as the Spirit moved them. The resulting Book is unique, inspired, infallible, inerrant, never-failing, ever-reviving, as old

as antiquity, as relevant as tomorrow's headlines, and forever established in heaven.

So why don't we read it more? A recent survey reported that 66 percent of the population agrees that the Bible contains everything we need to know for a meaningful life. But according to another poll, only nineteen percent read the Bible daily.

Perhaps we're overwhelmed with its contents, thinking, "I just don't understand the Bible. It's confusing. I don't know how it's put together or what it means."

Well, here's a resource to help, whether you're new to God's Word or a veteran student. The following pages provide the brief summary of each book in the Bible—Genesis to Revelation—what it means and what it means to you. These sixty-six digests give you each book in a nutshell, whether you're visiting well-known locations like John and Romans or seldom-visited sites like Jude, Obadiah, or Leviticus.

Jesus said we shouldn't live by bread alone, but by every word that proceeds from the mouth of God. He could have said, "every book," for God has divided His lessons to us into sixty-six segments—none of which should be missed. May blessings abound to you times sixty-six as you open and obey God's Word day by day!

BOOKS OF THE
OLD TESTAMENT

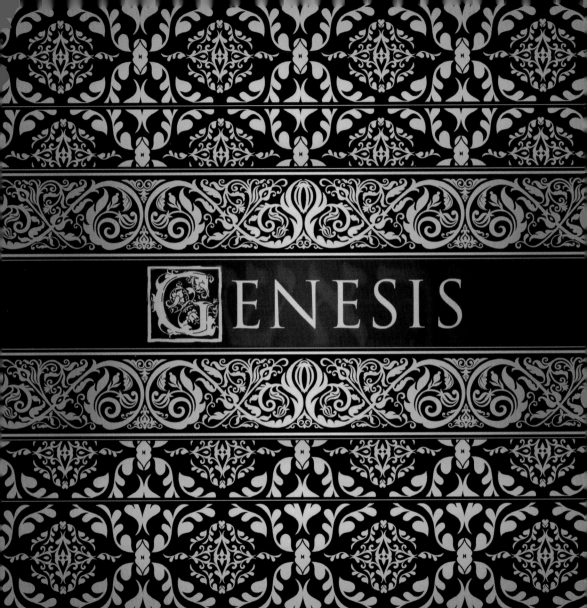

Many of our modern words like *genes*, *genetics*, *generations*, and *genealogy*, come from the same root word as *Genesis*, meaning *origin* or *creation*. The book of Genesis reveals our beginnings. Here we have the beginnings of the universe, of the human race, of sin; the beginning of God's program of redemption and of the Jewish people, who were the ones through whom God would bring the Messiah into the world.

The first eleven chapters of Genesis focus on primeval history, while the rest of the book gives patriarchal history—the story of Abraham and his descendants. Genesis 1 through 11 describes four great events: The Creation, the Fall, the Flood, and the Tower of Babel, while Genesis 12 through 50 tell of four great persons—Abraham, Isaac, Jacob, and Joseph.

The book of Genesis sets the stage for the entire biblical story and provides foundational lessons for us. As we read Genesis, we're reminded that no matter what life brings or how evil intrudes, God has a plan; and His ultimate plan cannot be frustrated. Many of the events recorded in Genesis permanently affected life on earth. Yet in spite of those epic events, God's plan remained on schedule. We can trust His ability to make sense of our lives even if our world appears to be upside down. When we read the book of Genesis, we're reminded that our Creator-God is sovereign and He is always in control—from beginning to end, from Genesis to Revelation.

KEY THOUGHT:

God is the origin of all things—the universe, the earth, life, humanity, the Jewish people, and the plan of redemption.

KEY VERSES:

"As for you, you meant evil against me;
but God meant it for good, in order to bring it
about as *it is* this day, to save many people alive.
Now therefore, do not be afraid."
Genesis 50:20-21

KEY ACTION:

Remember that no matter what life brings or how evil
intrudes, our Creator has a plan, His sovereignty cannot
be thwarted, and His plan is right on schedule.

KEY PRAYER:

Lord, help me to remember that You are in control
of my life, from the beginning to the end.

EXODUS

If you've ever booked a tour while traveling, you know everything depends on the skill of the guide. With a good guide, the trip is a pleasure. Inferior guides babble all day and may even get us lost. The book of Exodus tells us we have a Guide who provides authoritative commentary on life and goes before us every step of the way.

As the book of Genesis ends, Jacob and his family of about seventy souls are living in Egypt, where they found safety and relief from famine in the days of Joseph. But Exodus fast-forwards the story, and in the intervening years, the Israelites multiply into a mighty nation and are enslaved by the Egyptians. Exodus is the story of how God, using His servant Moses, delivered His people, crossed the Red Sea, traveled to Mount Sinai for further instructions, and built the tabernacle as a dwelling for God's guiding presence among them.

Exodus portrays the doctrine of redemption, even as the

Passover Lamb is a type of Christ. That elaborate tent, the tabernacle, also wonderfully foreshadows Jesus, the One who tabernacles among His people, leading us unfailingly.

Knowing that God goes ahead of us removes the fear that comes from dramatic changes in life. Our Redeemer has promised to guide our steps and give us the wisdom we need, but we must first set aside anxiety, quiet our hearts, and set our minds on seeking His will and His timing.

He knows the way through the wilderness.

KEY THOUGHT:

God provides the redemption, provision,
and guidance His people need.

KEY VERSE:

"Do not be afraid. Stand still, and see the salvation of the LORD, which He will accomplish for you today."
Exodus 14:13

KEY ACTION:

We must be still in God's presence, then go forward in God's power (see Exodus 14:13, 15).

KEY PRAYER:

Lord, help me to stand firm and see Your deliverance, for I know You will fight for me; I only need to be still.

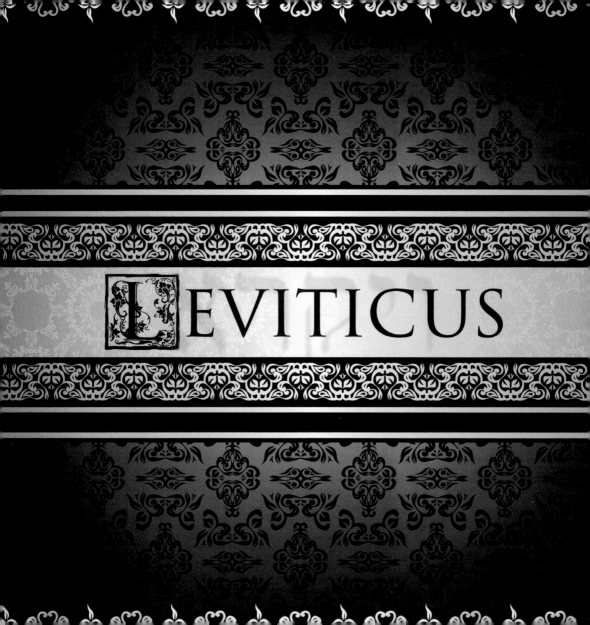

LEVITICUS

Many who try to read through the Bible hit a roadblock at Leviticus. Most preachers and teachers avoid the book too, making Leviticus one of the most underappreciated books in the Bible. That is, until you get to know it better and to value its resplendent theme of holiness.

It's helpful to know the background of this book. In the sunbaked wilderness of Sinai, Moses wanted to tell the children of Israel why they were there and how they should live. His explanation began in Exodus and continued into Leviticus, where the heart of the matter was revealed. God had chosen Israel as a distinct people to bless the nations, but they were required to be holy.

Leviticus concerns the responsibilities and duties of the Levites in their role as intermediaries between the people and God. The necessary instructions on how to worship—ceremonies, rituals, sacrifices, washings, offerings, and festivals—are all here, all of them symbols, items, occasions, and events portraying aspects of God's holiness, of human holiness, and of the Holy One to come—the Lord Jesus.

It wasn't easy to teach the Israelites about God's holiness, nor do *we* learn those lessons quickly. Even though we have God's Spirit within us, we must often be reminded of His nearness. We need to cultivate a sense of His presence and cleanse ourselves from all filthiness of the flesh and spirit, perfecting holiness in the fear of God. That's the theme of Leviticus, and it's a message well worth studying.

KEY THOUGHT:

God expects His people to reflect His holiness,
not just in rituals but in reality.

KEY VERSE:

"For I *am* the LORD your God.
You shall therefore consecrate yourselves,
and you shall be holy; for I *am* holy."
Leviticus 11:44

KEY ACTION:

Whenever sin occurs in life, we should
confess it promptly, consecrate ourselves
anew, and remain committed to
personal holiness.

KEY PRAYER:

Dear Father, may I be a reflection of Your
holiness, not just in thought, but in deed.

NUMBERS

A tragic story recently unfolded in Maine. Two hikers, rescued after getting lost in a state park, got in their car and drove away. But in the foggy darkness they took a wrong turn, drove down a boat ramp, and plunged into the ocean. By the time rescuers arrived it was too late.

There's nothing worse than taking a wrong turn, and that's a key message in the book of Numbers. Somehow on the way to the Promised Land, the Israelites took a wrong turn, and a one-month journey became a forty-year trek.

As you study Numbers, you can divide the book by its two numberings or censuses—one census of the Exodus generation and the other of the generation about to enter Canaan. Between these two events, an incredible story unfolds around several great themes: The covenant with its regulations; the land promised to Abraham and his descendants; and the promises of God, which are never invalidated by human failure. The greatest lesson in Numbers involves the crisis of faith that occurred when the Israelites believed the ten faithless spies instead of listening to Joshua and Caleb. The nation panicked in the desert, and their unbelieving hearts represented nothing less than rebellion against God.

Numbers warns us against taking the wrong turn of unbelief. We should listen to the Joshuas and Calebs in our lives and trust God's Word even when challenges loom. His promises are as sure as His power, and His peace is as near as His presence.

KEY THOUGHT:

There's nothing worse than taking a wrong turn
into the land of unbelief, for God wants to
lead us forward by faith.

KEY VERSES:

"The LORD bless you and keep you;
the LORD make His face shine upon you,
and be gracious to you; The LORD lift up His
countenance upon you, and give you peace."
Numbers 6:24-26

KEY ACTION:

Trust God's Word even when challenges loom,
for His promises are as secure as His power.

KEY PRAYER:

O Lord, keep me from fearing the
way ahead and rebelling against
You in unbelief.

DEUTERONOMY

Many of us are alarmed at reports showing steep declines of faith among our young people. It's increasingly hard to raise godly children in a godless world. Moses was no less concerned for the young people of his day. Near the end of his life, he delivered a series of sermons to teach the new generation—those about to enter Canaan—about the covenant of the Lord.

Except for Joshua and Caleb, the older generation had perished in the wilderness. Those who had been children during the Exodus were now ready to follow Joshua across the Jordan; but before Moses passed the reigns of leadership, he had a final opportunity to explain the Word of God to the Israelites. The word "Deuteronomy" means the retelling or second giving of the Law. The first twenty-six chapters of this book contain the introduction, background, and requirements of the covenant. Chapters 27 through 30 give the curses and blessings of the covenant. The final four chapters relate the transfer of leadership from Moses to Joshua.

It's summed up in chapter 6, when Moses gives timeless instruction about instilling faith within our children: *Love the LORD your God with all your heart, with all your soul, and with all your strength. And these words which I command you today shall be in your heart. You shall teach them diligently to your children, and talk of them when you sit in your house, when you walk by the way, when you lie down, and when you rise up.*

KEY THOUGHT:

Every new generation needs to learn
the lessons of the Lord and develop
a heritage of faith and obedience.

KEY VERSES:

"Hear, O Israel: the LORD our God,
the LORD is one! You shall love the LORD your
God with all your heart, with all your soul, and
with all your strength."
Deuteronomy 6:4-5

KEY ACTION:

Share the truth of God with your
children, with your grandchildren,
and with the generation to come
(see Deuteronomy 6:7).

KEY PRAYER:

Lord, You are my eternal God and my refuge,
and underneath me are the everlasting arms.

JOSHUA

onathan Swift, author of *Gulliver's Travels*, once quipped, "Promises and pie-crust are made to be broken." We've all heard enough political promises in our lives to share his cynicism. But the theme of Joshua tells us that God is utterly faithful to His promises, for His Word cannot be broken. As Joshua himself said late in life: "Not a word failed of any good thing which the Lord had spoken to Israel. All came to pass" (Joshua 21:45).

Joshua was born and raised in Egypt. He was a young man when he watched the contest between Moses and Pharaoh and the parting of the Red Sea. Moses later appointed Joshua head of the Hebrew army; and after the death of Moses, Joshua assumed leadership of Israel. The book of Joshua is the story of how he led God's people to possess the Promised Land.

Joshua's book tells this story in four phases. Chapters 1 through 5: Entering the land. Chapters 6 through 12:

Conquering the land. Chapters 13 through 21: Dividing the land. Chapters 22 through 24: Beginning life as one nation under God.

The theme through it all is: Yahweh is a promise-keeping God, therefore we're to live courageously. I don't know about you, but I'm strengthened whenever I read the opening chapter of this book, as the Lord tells us: "I will not leave you nor forsake you (Joshua 1:4). "Be strong and of good courage . . . Do not be afraid, nor be dismayed, for the Lord your God is with you wherever you go" (Joshua 1:9).

KEY THOUGHT:

Yahweh is a promise-keeping God who leads His children through warfare to victory, just as He gave the Israelites the land promised to Abraham and his descendants.

KEY VERSE:

"Be strong and very courageous, that you may
observe to do according to all the law which Moses
My servant commanded you; do not turn from it
to the right hand or to the left, that you may
prosper wherever you go."
Joshua 1:7

KEY ACTION:

"As for me and my house,
we will serve the LORD."
Joshua 24:15

KEY PRAYER:

God, thank you for the assurance that You
will never leave us nor forsake us.

JUDGES

Have you ever heard the phrase: "Christianity is just one generation from extinction"? When we read Judges, we see how easily the heritage of faith can be fumbled from one generation to the next. Judges 2 says that after the Israelites conquered and possessed the land, everyone went to his own area and the people served the Lord throughout the lifetime of Joshua. But after Joshua's generation passed away, "another generation grew up who knew neither the Lord nor what He had done for Israel" (Judges 2:10, NIV).

There resulted a series of sin cycles—sin, judgment, cries for help, and deliverance. The people would fall into sin, fall prey to their enemies, and cry out to God; and God in His mercy would send a judge or a deliverer like Gideon, Samson, Jephthah, or Deborah. Their influence would last awhile, then the whole process would repeat itself. This repetitive pattern in Judges conveys a powerful lesson: To the very utmost of our ability we must focus our energy on raising our children in the nurture and instruction of the Lord, teaching them the truths of Scripture and giving them testimonies of faith.

KEY THOUGHT:

When generations arise without a knowledge of God and His commands, they fall into a downward spiral of sin, defeat, judgment, and despair.

KEY VERSE:

"Nevertheless, the LORD raised up judges
who delivered them out of the hand of
those who plundered them."
Judges 2:16

KEY ACTION:

We must break the cycle of apathy, sin, ruin,
defeat, and despair with the power of lasting
repentance and revival.

KEY PRAYER:

Lord of my heart, may You vanquish my foes. I will find
strength in my love for You, and Your love for me.

RUTH

What makes a good movie or novel? What about tragedy, death, loyalty, vivid characters, abiding love, and a happy ending? That's the book of Ruth, the Bible's classic love story, a timeless and true tale of ruin and redemption.

The opening line of Ruth is a snapshot of Israel during the time of the judges: "Now it came to pass, in the days when the judges ruled, that there was a famine in the land" (Ruth 1:1). This famine drove an Israelite family from Bethlehem to the nation of Moab, where the men of the family died. The surviving widow, Naomi, and her daughter-in-law, Ruth, returned bitterly to Bethlehem where God, in His providence, brought a loving man into their life—a wealthy landowner named Boaz, who redeemed and married Ruth.

From start to finish, Ruth's story is about redemption. The Hebrew words for "redeem" and "redemption" occur over twenty times in this book. Boaz became a picture of the redemption offered by Christ. By her acceptance of Naomi's God, Ruth became a picture of what Paul would teach centuries later: it's not by physical descent from Abraham that one is redeemed, but by the *faith* of Abraham.

Ruth shows us the importance of both human and divine love. This four-chapter book teaches us to trust God who redeems the hardships of our past and who also provides for the needs of the present moment. We can entrust the future results of our day-to-day decisions to Him, who is our Kinsman-Redeemer.

KEY THOUGHT:

In Boaz, God provided Ruth a kinsman-redeemer who exchanged her bitterness for blessing and foreshadowed the redemptive work of the coming Kinsman-Redeemer, Jesus Christ.

KEY VERSE:

"Entreat me not to leave you, *or to* turn
back from following after you; for wherever you go,
I will go; and wherever you lodge, I will lodge; your
people *shall be* my people, and your God, my God."
Ruth 1:16

KEY ACTION:

Trust in the God who redeems the hardships of our
past, blesses us now, and provides for our future.

KEY PRAYER:

God, I ask You to renew my life and sustain me in
old age that I might praise the Lord who has not
left me without a Guardian or Redeemer.

I SAMUEL

Thomas Carlyle famously said: "The history of the world is but the biography of great men." Many people dislike history, considering it nothing but cold facts, impersonal dates, and lists of events. But the lives of those who shaped history give us some of the richest stories in the world.

God used the biographical method in giving us the story of Old Testament history, and 1 Samuel is a prime example. It tells Israel's story through the lives of three leaders: Samuel, Saul, and David. Each life is a lesson for the rest of us, and the themes of 1 Samuel are for Christians in every station of life.

The first part of the book is devoted to the story of Samuel, the boy who said, "Speak for Your servant hears," (1 Samuel 3:10), and the man who became the last of the judges of Israel. The middle part of the book is about Saul, Israel's first king, who started with great promise and ended with tragic sorrow. The last part of the book centers on David, the youngest son in a shepherding family who became a man after God's own heart.

As we read this book, it's helpful to remember we're all biographers. Each of us is writing the record of our own lives, and one day soon the story will be complete. Popularity and image will fade away; but those after God's own heart will leave a legacy of leadership that will endure until the Lord returns.

KEY THOUGHT:

The stories of Samuel, Saul, and David remind us that popularity and image will fade away; but those after God's own heart will leave a legacy of leadership.

KEY VERSE:

"Has the LORD *as great* delight in burnt offerings
and sacrifices, as in obeying the voice of the LORD?
Behold, to obey is better than sacrifice, *and* to
heed than the fat of rams."
1 Samuel 15:22

KEY ACTION:

Don't judge by first impressions, for God doesn't look at
people as we do; we look at the external appearance,
but God looks at the heart (see 1 Samuel 16:7).

KEY PRAYER:

Lord, as I face giants in my life,
remind me that You do not save by
sword and spear, but by Your own
power; for the battle is Yours.

II SAMUEL

areer experts frequently tell us to follow our passion, but sometimes that's the surest way to fail. Our passions can get us into a lot of trouble. It's much better to follow God's guidance every step of the way. That's the lesson of the book of 2 Samuel, which is the story of David as king of Israel.

This book begins with David's ascension to the throne. It goes on to describe his royal accomplishments and moral failures. At the end of the book we have his final words and deeds. David was a shepherd who became the ruler of God's people. His reign was a monarchy under a theocratic umbrella, one that established a line of kings culminating in the King of Kings, Jesus Christ. One of the themes of this book is the Davidic Covenant, which guarantees the perpetual nature of David's dynasty leading to the Messiah, the Anointed King to come. Woven into the story is the theme of grace. Despite David's failures, God forgave him, continued the covenant, and worked it all for good because David was a man after God's own heart.

Second Samuel is a prolonged warning about the subtle nature of our passions. Every day presents new temptations and dangers, as David encountered with Bathsheba. We need God's abiding wisdom, protection, and companionship. As we acknowledge His kingship over our lives, we have the promise that His hand will uphold us and that He will guide us every step along the way.

KEY THOUGHT:

We must follow God's guidance rather than our own passions, at every step.

KEY VERSES:

"You are God, and Your words are true, and You have promised this goodness to Your servant. Now therefore, let it please You to bless the house of Your servant, that it may continue before You forever."
2 Samuel 7:28-29

KEY ACTION:

Acknowledge God's kingship
in every area of life.

KEY PRAYER:

Lord, I praise You because You reign!
You are the Rock of my salvation.

I KINGS

Here's a Scripture trivia question: Who was the first person in the Bible to raise the dead, though he himself never died? And though he's the most frequently mentioned prophet in Scripture, he didn't write one word of the Bible. The answer is . . . Elijah—the rugged prophet who dominates much of 1 Kings.

The books of 1 and 2 Kings—one long book in the Hebrew— open with the story of how God blessed Israel during the days of Solomon, yet how the nation split apart and declined after Solomon's death. As you read 1 Kings, notice that chapters 1 through 11 describe the glory of Solomon's reign, but the remaining chapters tell of the growing failures of the successive kings in both North and South. Despite occasional lurches toward obedience, the priests, princes, and people of God spiraled downward like water through a drain until both nations were wiped away by neighboring empires.

Throughout the story, Elijah and his fellow prophets—men like Nathan, Ahijah, and Jehu—vainly called their nations to repentance. God's people today are still warning, cautioning, and proclaiming His message. At times, like Elijah, we see little outward success. But there's never reason to be discouraged where God is concerned. In reading 1 Kings, we learn that even the downward twists and turns of history serve the ultimate purposes of God, and the story of Elijah and his times reminds us that God is still on His throne as king of Israel and as Lord of all.

KEY THOUGHT:

The decline of Israel during and after the days of Solomon warns us of the dangers of complacency, but also teaches us to practice the boldness of Elijah.

KEY VERSE:

"Keep the charge of the LORD your God: to walk in His ways, to keep His statutes, His commandments, His judgments, and His testimonies, as it is written in the Law of Moses, that you may prosper in all that you do and wherever you turn."
1 Kings 2:3

KEY ACTION:

We must be as cautious in times of prosperity as in times of peril, lest we relax our guard as Solomon did and allow our spiritual passion to grow lukewarm.

KEY PRAYER:

Lord, give me a wise and discerning heart to govern my life and distinguish between right and wrong.

II KINGS

Television gives us around-the-clock news, but it's a mixed blessing. A constant diet of current events can leave us in a state of nervous depression. Well, imagine following the news from ancient Israel during the days of the Old Testament kings! The God-fearing people of those days must have struggled mightily to maintain their morale amid the downward spiral of their times. The book of 2 Kings is like a news account of this discouraging succession of kings, starting with evil King Ahab. The first seventeen chapters of the book describe the events that occurred in the days of the divided kingdoms of Israel and Judah; the final eight chapters focus on Judah alone. The story concludes with Israel exiled in Assyria and Judah banished to Babylon.

It would be easy, reading all this, to close the book and sigh, "All is lost!" Yet throughout the story in 2 Kings, God never lost control of Israel's destiny, and His promises were undeterred. Even the fall of Judah, as tragic as it was, set the stage for subsequent events in Old Testament and Intertestamental times, leading to the birth of Jesus Christ, the Son of Abraham, the Son of David.

Yes, we need to keep up with current events; but don't let the bad news of earth get you down. Focus on the Good News of Jesus Christ. Kings may fail and nations may falter, but God is still on His throne, and His rule will have no end.

KEY THOUGHT:

Though the story of the decline and fall of
Israel's monarchy appears bleak at times,
God never lost control of Israel's destiny
and His promises were undeterred.

KEY VERSE:

"So he answered, 'Do not fear,
for those who *are* with us *are* more
than those who *are* with them.'"
2 Kings 6:16

KEY ACTION:

We, like Elisha, should live with confidence in chaotic
times, for we are protected by the invisible armies of
the Lord of Hosts (see 2 Kings 6:17).

KEY PRAYER:

Lord, may a double portion of
Your Spirit be upon me.

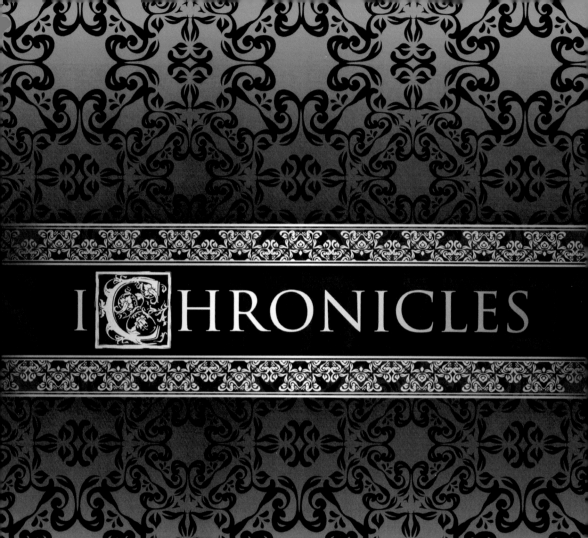

I Chronicles

One of life's great tragedies is the loss of memory. When people suffer dementia, they lose touch with their past; in doing so they lose hope in their future.

The book of 1 Chronicles was written to keep the post-exilic Israelites from suffering spiritual dementia by providing a summary of their history. It gave their collective memory both a heritage and a hope.

According to tradition, the author of 1 and 2 Chronicles was Ezra, and he wrote these books to reassure the returning exiles that God was still at work in the promises He had given. These exiles had few personal recollections of the days before the Assyrian and Babylonian invasions. They had never seen the glorious temple of Solomon. They had never experienced the shoulder-to-shoulder crowds in Jerusalem during the feasts. And so someone—Ezra maybe—compiled a history for the returning exiles. If 1 and 2 Kings were written to explain why the nation was exiled, 1 and 2 Chronicles were written to explain that the returning exiles were still the people of God. The first chapters of this book provide genealogies proving they were indeed heirs of the promises. The rest of the book is about David's reign, Solomon's Temple, and the Davidic Covenant promising a perpetual throne to Israel.

As you study 1 Chronicles, remember the heritage God has given you. The Bible frequently warns against forgetting what He has done; for in our heritage—in our own chronicles—are the keys to our future.

KEY THOUGHT:

God's covenant to David and His promises
to Israel are perpetual, designed to give
His people a heritage and a future.

KEY VERSE:

"Set your heart and your soul to seek the LORD your God. Therefore arise and build the sanctuary of the LORD God, to bring the ark of the covenant of the LORD and the holy articles of God into the house that is to be built for the name of the LORD."
1 Chronicles 22:19

KEY ACTION:

Crown the Lord as King, and joyfully labor in the service of His work.

KEY PRAYER:

Lord, help me to remain strong and courageous, trusting my future in Your hands.

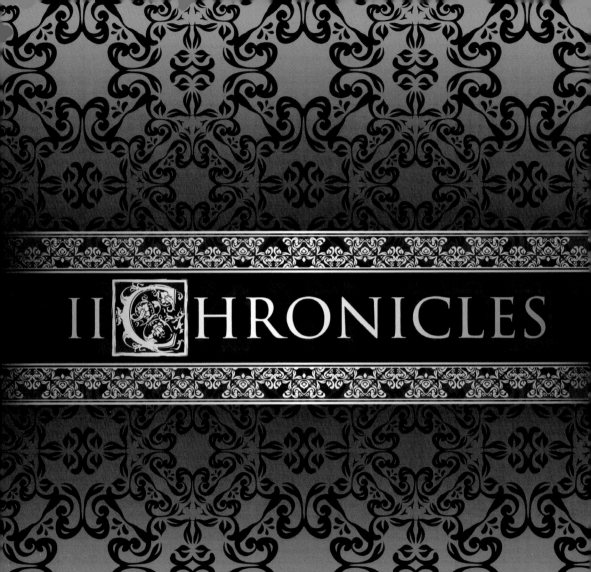

II CHRONICLES

f you've ever gone through a ground-shifting change in life, you know it can be unsettling and upsetting. That's how God's people felt in 2 Chronicles as they returned home after seventy years in captivity. They were a people in transition and needed an explanation of their past and future. Second Chronicles met that need by focusing post-exilic Israel on its heritage and hope, especially as symbolized by the temple in Jerusalem. Terms like *temple* and *the house of the LORD* occur 139 times in 2 Chronicles. Nothing symbolized God's presence among His people more than the temple.

This book tells stories about Solomon, who built the original temple; about Hezekiah, who repaired the temple; and about Josiah, who purified the temple following days of idolatry. During the final years of Judah the temple was plundered and destroyed; but seventy years later a decree went forth to rebuild the temple as a sign of God's enduring care for His people.

While God no longer dwells in a physical temple of stone, the New Testament declares that a believer's body and spirit is a temple where He resides. We are bought at a price; therefore, we're to glorify God in our body and spirit, which are His. In today's terms, Solomon's temple cost hundreds of millions of dollars to build. Yet God purchased each of us with something far more valuable—the precious blood of Christ. Let's glorify Him as His temples, houses of His glory, vessels fit for the Master's use.

KEY THOUGHT:

God is determined to have a temple,
a dwelling place for His glory on earth.

KEY VERSE:

"Thus says Cyrus king of Persia:
All the kingdoms of the earth the LORD
God of heaven has given me. And He
has commanded me to build Him a
house at Jerusalem which is in Judah.
Who *is* among you of all His people?
May the LORD his God *be* with him,
and let him go up!"
2 Chronicles 36:23

KEY ACTION:

Glorify God in the temple where He
resides—in your body and spirit.

KEY PRAYER:

O God, when trouble comes,
help me keep my eyes focused on You!

Rebuilding is usually harder than original construction, whether it's a coach rebuilding a team, a family rebuilding a home, a couple rebuilding a marriage, or a prodigal rebuilding a life. But whatever we're rebuilding, we have a blueprint for it in the book of Ezra.

Years after the Jewish people had been defeated and dispersed by their enemies, a group of Jews, in three waves over a period of about a hundred years, returned to their ancestral homeland to rebuild their nation. It was a tough trip. Their once-glorious temple was in total ruin and the wall around the city was rubble. The book of Ezra tells us how these returnees rebuilt the temple; and the book of Nehemiah tells how they rebuilt the walls.

Ezra falls into two sections that cover the first and second returns of these exiles. Chapters 1 through 6 describe the first group of returnees and the rebuilding of the temple. Chapters 7 through 10 cover the second return and the ministry of the teacher Ezra, who taught the people God's Word and stressed the importance of remaining separate from the world.

The book of Ezra teaches us to seek the Lord in prayer, submit to His Word, and acknowledge His wisdom, power, presence, and love. The rubble may not be cleared away in a day or a year, but when we put first things first, the rest of life will come back into alignment. Begin with the altar—with worship—and restoration will follow.

KEY THOUGHT:

In showing how the returning exiles rebuilt their temple, city, and nation, Ezra teaches us to rebuild areas in our lives that have been damaged or defeated.

KEY VERSE:

"Then I proclaimed a fast there at the river of Ahava, that we might humble ourselves before our God, to seek from Him the right way for us and our little ones and all our possessions."
Ezra 8:21

KEY ACTION:

In rebuilding anything, we must start with the altar—reestablishing the Cross of Jesus Christ as central to our lives and activities.

KEY PRAYER:

Lord, may I be faithful to study Your Word and live my life as a testimony to its precepts.

NEHEMIAH

There's no shortage of leadership books in the marketplace. Amazon lists over 100,000 books on the subject, with more published every day. Few of them are as practical and up-to-date as the book of Nehemiah. None of them have the inspired power that resides in the thirteen chapters of this book, which is located near the end of the Old Testament historical books.

Nehemiah, who lived in the fifth century B.C., was born among the exiles of Judah. Many years earlier, his people had been defeated and deported; but Nehemiah's leadership abilities placed him in the service of the most powerful king on earth, Artaxerxes of Persia. As the book opens, Nehemiah received a report from his ancestral city, Jerusalem. The walls there were broken down, the gates were burned with fire, and the survivors were in distress. God deeply burdened Nehemiah with the plight of Jerusalem, and within four verses of the beginning of the book, the reader finds Nehemiah weeping, mourning, fasting, and praying. With the king's permission, Nehemiah traveled to Jerusalem to oversee the rebuilding of the walls of the ancient capital of his people.

As we read the book of Nehemiah, we can't help learning vital skills of leadership. This book gives us one of Scripture's best case-studies in spiritual and visionary oversight—setting goals, planning projects, delegating tasks, organizing people, solving problems, and accomplishing results.

One person empowered by God can make a difference—whether that person is Nehemiah or whether that person is you.

KEY THOUGHT:

One person like Nehemiah, blessed by God
with passion and leadership, can make a
difference for time and eternity.

KEY VERSES:

"So the wall was finished . . . . And it happened, when all our enemies heard *of it*, and all the nations around us saw *these things*, that they were very disheartened in their own eyes; for they perceived that this work was done by our God."
Nehemiah 6:15-16

KEY ACTION:

All of us can become better leaders by studying the life and methods of Nehemiah.

KEY PRAYER:

Father, do Your perfect work in me that You might find me a faithful servant who leads others to You.

ESTHER

The words of an old hymn say: "Build your hopes on things eternal, hold to God's unchanging hand." Another song speaks of being guided by God's "unseen hand." Well, with the book of Esther we have the only book of the Bible containing no reference to God's name; yet His unchanging, unseen hand cannot be missed.

Esther, the last of the historical books of the Old Testament, tells a dramatic story of a woman caught up in a battle for the survival of the Jewish people. During the days of the Persian Empire, an egomaniacal, high-ranking official named Haman hatched a plan to exterminate all the Jews on earth. What followed was one of history's most intrigue-filled accounts of political maneuverings, death threats, shocking plot-twists, and dramatic rescues. At the center of the action was Queen Esther, who had risen to the throne "for such a time as this" (Esther 4:14). Guided by her relative Mordecai, Esther turned the tables on Haman, and the villain was hanged on the very gallows he had prepared for Mordecai.

The book of Esther shows how God's unseen hand orchestrated the affairs of humanity by providential arrangement. Esther teaches that God purposely guides our steps even when we're not aware of it and even when things don't make sense. Every thread woven into the fabric of the Christian life is part of the ultimate tapestry that someday we'll view in glory. We really can build our hopes on things eternal as we hold to God's unchanging hand.

KEY THOUGHT:

With His hidden hand of providence,
God purposely guides and protects His
people, even when they're unaware of it
and even when, as in the days of
Mordecai and Esther, disaster looms.

KEY VERSE:

"Yet who knows whether you have come
to the kingdom for *such* a time as this?"
Esther 4:14

KEY ACTION:

Trust the hidden resolutions of God's
providence when you can't see visible
solutions to life's dilemmas.

KEY PRAYER:

Lord, may I be sold out to Your cause!
May I be found worthy to be used by You
in a special and unique way.

JOB

Apologist William Lane Craig observed, "No logical inconsistency has ever been demonstrated between the two statements 'God exists' and 'evil exists.'" In fact, the presence of evil actually demonstrates God's existence because without God there would be no moral foundation for calling anything evil.

He's right. Nevertheless the question of evil still vexes us, and it is difficult to explain the presence of suffering in the world. All of us occasionally ask the question "Why?" The book of Job addresses this issue head-on. As the book opens we learn about *human suffering*, but by its conclusion we also learn a great deal about *God's sovereignty*.

The outline of Job is easy to follow. The first two chapters are Prologue, in which we're introduced to Job and his disasters. Chapters 3 through 27 are Dialogues, in which his friends reasoned with him about his suffering and suggested he had committed secret but serious sins. Chapters 28 through 42 are a set of Monologues, mainly by Job and God. And the final paragraphs of the book comprise an Epilogue, in which Job's problems are resolved and his wisdom deepened.

Righteous people like Job *do* sometimes suffer, and the devil himself is often behind our troubles. But God *can* be trusted, and we must learn to walk by faith rather than sight. If you're facing difficulty today, remember the statements of Job—words of sheer but splendid faith: "Though He slay me, yet will I trust Him . . . I know that my Redeemer lives" (Job 13:15; 19:25).

KEY THOUGHT:

Those who turn fully to God in sorrow—even if they argue, plead, and protest in His presence as Job did— will find a pathway to the tender mercies of heaven.

KEY VERSE:

"For I know *that* my Redeemer lives,
and He shall stand at last on the earth."
Job 19:25

KEY ACTION:

We must trust God even when it appears
He is slaying us (see Job 13:15).

KEY PRAYER:

Lord, whether You give or take away,
help me say, "Blessed be the name
of the Lord!"

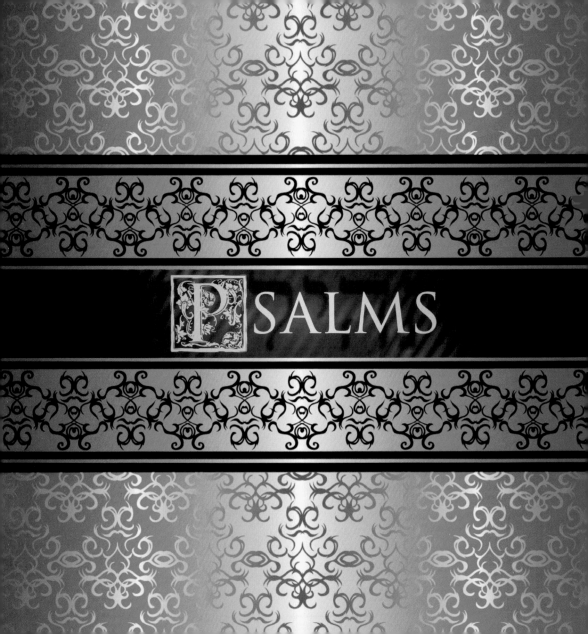

PSALMS

henever God's people gather, whether in grief or celebration, they sing. The style of music changes, but singing remains a deeply-rooted part of our heritage. From the spontaneous choir at the Red Sea in Exodus 15 to the professional choirs David assembled among the Levites, songs run through the Old Testament like musical ribbons. And in the middle of it all—at the very heart of the Bible—is the book of Psalms, the hymnbook of the people of God.

Psalms, the Bible's longest book, comprises five separate collections: Book 1 is chapters 1 through 41; Book 2 is chapters 42 through 72; Book 3 is chapters 73 through 89; Book 4 is chapters 90 through 106; and Book 5 is chapters 107 through 150. Each of these collections ends with an outburst of praise— an *Amen* or a *Hallelujah*.

Often when we cannot find words to express our fears, joys, longings, or sorrows. We find them in the pages of this book, as

Psalm 100 exhorts us:

Make a joyful shout to the LORD, all you lands! Serve the LORD with gladness; come before His presence with singing. Know that the LORD, He is God; it is He who has made us, and not we ourselves; we are His people and the sheep of His pasture. Enter into His gates with thanksgiving, and into His courts with praise. Be thankful to Him, and bless His name. For the LORD is good; His mercy is everlasting, and His truth endures to all generations.

KEY THOUGHT:

The book of Psalms—Israel's hymnbook—teaches us to continually praise God for His greatness, goodness, and glory.

KEY VERSES:

"Make a joyful shout to the LORD, all you lands!
Serve the LORD with gladness; come before
His presence with singing."
Psalm 100:1-2

KEY ACTION:

Worship! Sing! Praise!

KEY PRAYER:

In all things let my words and thoughts
honor You Lord. May my life be a
living praise to Your goodness!

ROVERBS

In life, skill is what distinguishes success from failure, victory from defeat, and excellence from mediocrity. And skill—or "wisdom," as the Hebrew is translated—is the overarching theme in the book of Proverbs.

In biblical times, wisdom was often passed from person to person through the use of proverbs—pithy sayings that typically capitalized on a comparison or contrast from everyday life. The master at creating these short sayings was Solomon—he spoke 3,000 proverbs during his reign. His wisdom was a gift from God in answer to prayer, and his wisdom is encapsulated in his proverbs. The book of Proverbs, written primarily by Solomon, was designed to produce a nation of people who were skilled at living a life consistent with God's spiritual and natural laws.

No book in the Bible sets forth its purpose with greater clarity than Proverbs. The opening paragraph tells us these Proverbs were given to teach us wisdom and instruction, to enable us to perceive words of understanding, and to give prudence to the simple, and knowledge and discretion to the young.

As we read through Proverbs, especially with the illumination of the Holy Spirit, we will learn wisdom—the skill of living—when it comes to relationships, finances, emotions, attitudes, integrity, marriage, and disciplines in every area of life. As Proverbs 1:7 tells us: *The fear of the LORD is the beginning of knowledge, but fools despise wisdom and instruction.*

KEY THOUGHT:

Success in the practical matters of life
requires reverence for God and
obedience to His rules for living.

KEY VERSE:

"The fear of the *LORD is* the
beginning of knowledge, *but* fools
despise wisdom and instruction."
Proverbs 1:7

KEY ACTION:

We must receive God's words and treasure
His commands within us, inclining our ears to wisdom
and our hearts to understanding (see Proverbs 2:1-2).

KEY PRAYER:

God, help me walk in the way of goodness
and keep to the paths of righteousness!

ECCLESIASTES

The *New York Times* recently reported on the upsurge of students in philosophy courses at major universities. According to the paper, young people are seeking philosophical answers to their growing confusion and disillusionment.

Well, they need to read Ecclesiastes, the Bible's built-in philosophy course, written by Solomon, the wisest man in the Old Testament. After a promising start, Solomon was drawn away from the Lord by the influence of his foreign wives. The resulting despair probably prompted him to write this book. We can track Solomon's spiritual and intellectual progress by reading all three of his books. Song of Solomon represents Solomon as a young king—virile, energetic, and full of zeal for God. Proverbs represents his mature years and sage advice. Ecclesiastes represents his sunset years as he looked back and realized his life was unfulfilled by money, possessions, education, or pleasure. The premise of Ecclesiastes is that life is meaningless unless God is acknowledged. God has put eternity in our hearts, and without eternal values we'll always be looking for substitutes. Everything under the sun is vanity and a chasing after the wind.

Ecclesiastes tells us: Without God life is as empty as the wind; but the fear of the Lord is a basis for wisdom and fulfillment, and that's the only sound philosophy in life. As Solomon sums up in Ecclesiastes 12:13: "Let us hear the conclusion of the whole matter: Fear God and keep His commandments, for this is the whole duty of man" (KJV).

KEY THOUGHT:

Life without God is meaningless.

KEY VERSE:

"Let us hear the conclusion of the whole matter: Fear God and keep His commandments, for this is man's all."
Ecclesiastes 12:13

KEY ACTION:

To be happy and fulfilled, we must fear God, obey Him, live for eternity, and let Him bring meaningfulness to every area of life.

KEY PRAYER:

Lord, please grant me wisdom from above that I may find true happiness and meaning in Your ways.

Song of Solomon

Every married couple needs a little getaway, a special place they enjoy revisiting. Well, there's such a place in the Bible. Almost hidden among the leaves of Scripture is a romantic getaway called "Song of Songs," celebrating the joy and genius of marriage.

Its author, Solomon, recorded a golden season in his life when he fell in love and married a young woman known only as "the Shulamite." This unlikely love story between a king and a commoner is a template for understanding that marriage was instituted by God for our joy.

The book is composed of fifteen reflections written as lyric poetry. Read them as pages from a love journal, brimming with insights about romance, marriage, and intimacy. Solomon and his bride plumbed the depths of their language to craft word pictures about love and marriage—and this has never been more timely. In a day when marriage is being redefined by contemporary culture, Song of Solomon reveals the lasting influence of a strong marriage on future generations. We can't allow resentments, selfishness, and neglect to nibble away at our homes. These are the "little foxes" that spoil the vines. Little things in marriage count in a big way. Little sins can produce big problems; but small acts of love can yield lasting blessings.

Some commentators feel Song of Solomon is an analogy of God's love for us; but its primary meaning is for marriage now, and it shows us how to keep romance alive in a loving home.

KEY THOUGHT:

God's pattern for courtship and marriage provides
a template for a beautiful and lasting relationship
based on His unquenchable love.

KEY VERSES:

"Set me as a seal upon your heart, as a seal upon
your arm; for love *is as* strong as death, jealousy *as*
cruel as the grave; its flames *are* flames of fire, a most
vehement flame. Many waters cannot quench love,
nor can the floods drown it."
Song of Solomon 8:6-7

KEY ACTION:

Never let resentments, arguments, neglect,
and other "little foxes" nibble away at the
health of the romance of the home.

KEY PRAYER:

Father, may I be loved purely
and learn to love purely.

ISAIAH

Have you ever in weakness found renewed strength through the words of a parent, spouse, or friend? The right words at the right time restore our courage and keep us from despair. That's how we feel as we read the words of Judah's greatest preacher—the prophet Isaiah. His words overflow with pathos and passion, whether he is talking about judgment, healing, or the majesty of God. Throughout the book there are so many references to the coming Messiah that Isaiah is sometimes called the Fifth Gospel.

Isaiah began ministering in Judah around 740 B.C. He witnessed the final years of the northern kingdom of Israel, and he warned his tiny nation of Judah and its capital, Jerusalem, of similar judgment. In the first part of the book, chapters 1 through 39, Isaiah spoke of judgment and hope, warning that just as God used Assyria to judge Israel, He would use Babylon to judge Judah. The last part of Isaiah, chapters 40 through 66, is full of

God's encouragement for the future exiles. These are some of the most comforting passages in the Bible.

Isaiah's words and predictions give us never-ending strength. If you're low today, listen to what Isaiah said in chapter 40, verses 30 and 31: "Even the youths shall faint and be weary, and the young men shall utterly fall, but those who wait on the Lord shall renew their strength; they shall mount up with wings like eagles, they shall run and not be weary; they shall walk and not faint."

KEY THOUGHT:

God is both our Majestic Lord
and our Suffering Servant, and by
waiting on Him we can renew our strength
(see Isaiah 6:1; 53:3; 40:31).

KEY VERSE:

"For *as* the heavens are higher than
the earth, so are My ways higher
than your ways, and My thoughts
than your thoughts."
Isaiah 55:9

KEY ACTION:

We need a revelation of God's glory
that makes us cry, "Here am I! Send me"
(see Isaiah 6:8).

KEY PRAYER:

Lord, may I be in perfect peace
because my mind is stayed on You.

JEREMIAH

The old Spiritual, "There Is a Balm in Gilead" says, "Sometimes I feel discouraged and think my work's in vain, but then the Holy Spirit revives my soul again." Discouragement is an occupational hazard of ministry; but whenever we're downcast, we can turn to Jeremiah—the Weeping Prophet—and regain our perspective.

When Jeremiah was commissioned, the Lord said to him, "Prepare yourself and arise, and speak to them all that I command you. Do not be dismayed . . . I have made you this day a fortified city and an iron pillar . . . They will fight against you, but they shall not prevail against you for I am with you" (Jeremiah 1:17-19).

Jeremiah's forty-year ministry was centered in Judah during the reigns of the final five kings of Judah, right up until the time Babylon destroyed the city. Jeremiah didn't have an easy task. He was beaten and imprisoned. He was thrown into a muddy cistern. His writings were cut up and burned. In the end, he was forcibly taken to Egypt, where he apparently died. But he was faithful at every point—sometimes weeping and struggling to understand—but faithful. And through him God gave the promise of establishing a "new covenant with the house of Israel and with the house of Judah" — a covenant fulfilled by the shed blood of Jesus.

When we do our best for the Lord and have little to show for it, we're companions with Jeremiah. Just as the Lord was with him, He will be with you. God will bless your efforts for His glory.

KEY THOUGHT:

God expects us to persevere in His work,
even when our heart is broken, our message
is rejected, and our labor appears vain.

KEY VERSE:

"Call to Me, and I will answer you,
and show you great and mighty
things, which you do not know."
Jeremiah 33:3

KEY ACTION:

We must go to all to whom He sends
us and speak whatever He tells us
(see Jeremiah 1:7).

KEY PRAYER:

Almighty Lord, remind me that
You are the potter and I am the clay.

LAMENTATIONS

Whether it's Hank Williams singing, "I'm So Lonesome I Could Cry," or the Beatles yearning for "Yesterday," there's something about sad songs that summarizes the emotions of millions of people. Well, the saddest songs ever written are in the book of Lamentations.

After the Babylonian invasion in 586 B.C., the land of Israel was reduced to rubble. Jerusalem was in ruins, the temple obliterated, the city walls flattened, and the people massacred or deported. The prophet Jeremiah, melancholy by nature, was broken by the devastation. He had devoted a lifetime to urging his people to repent, and his book of Lamentations is a funeral dirge for Jerusalem following the judgment that fell on them.

Like the Psalms that served as Israel's hymnbook, the five laments of Jeremiah are musical in nature, thus emotional. They're carefully crafted as alphabetic acrostics, meaning the verses begin with successive letters of the Hebrew alphabet. There are five chapters and five laments. Chapter 1 details Jerusalem's desolation. Chapter 2 characterizes God's anger against His people and their response. Chapter 3 documents Judah's complaint against what God has done. Lament 4 contrasts Judah's past and present. The fifth chapter stresses repentance and forgiveness.

Despite the sorrow in this book, our eyes are drawn to the hope it contains. In Lamentations 3, these words are like shafts of sunlight breaking through the clouds: *Through the LORD's mercies we are not consumed, because His compassions fail not. They are new every morning; great is Your faithfulness.*

KEY THOUGHT:

Sinfulness brings inevitable sorrow and judgment,
but even in lamentable times God is faithful
and His compassions never fail.

KEY VERSES:

"*Through* the LORD's mercies we are
not consumed, because His compassions
fail not. *They are* new every morning;
great *is* Your faithfulness."
Lamentations 3:22-23

KEY ACTION:

Just like Jeremiah in distress, we must
lift our thoughts from the ashes and
throw open the windows of our minds,
recalling the wonders of the God in
whom we hope.

KEY PRAYER:

God, give me patience to faithfully
and joyfully wait upon You.

EZEKIEL

Do you remember the saying, Disappointments are God's appointments? That's true for every child of God, though it's hard to remember when disappointments land on our doorstep.

Ezekiel was a young man who faced life-altering disappointment. He'd prepared all his life to serve as a temple priest, but before his service began he was deported and exiled from Judah—one of thousands displaced by Babylon in 597 B.C. We can't imagine the young man's distress; but at the beginning of the book, heaven opened and Ezekiel saw visions of the glory of God. And God in His glory appointed Ezekiel to prophetic service. Rather than being a priest in Jerusalem, he became a prophet to the expatriates in Babylon, and this book is the record of his life and ministry.

Ezekiel's visions and verses are timeless—the opening vision of the wheels within the wheels; the subsequent vision of the glory of God departing the temple; or, later on, the vision of the Valley of Dry Bones, the vision of Gog and Magog, and the incredible tour of the restored temple given in the final chapters of the book. Only the visions of Daniel and John equal the intensity of those in Ezekiel. They mesmerize us to this day, and the message of Ezekiel adds tremendously to our understanding of the present and future.

For God's children, disappointments truly are His appointments; and you can count on it: If one door closes, it's because God intends to open another.

KEY THOUGHT:

God has a vision for our future, even when it appears we've been exiled in a land of failure.

KEY VERSE:

"I will put My Spirit within you and cause
you to walk in My statutes, and you will
keep My judgments and do *them*."
Ezekiel 36:27

KEY ACTION:

We must speak God's words to our generation, whether
they hear or whether they refuse (see Ezekiel 2:7).

KEY PRAYER:

Lord, allow me to stand in the gap.
Let me be the answer to a need!

DANIEL

In the years leading to the Second World War, Winston Churchill often complained that Parliament wasn't taking Hitler's threats seriously enough, and Churchill sometimes quoted a little poem that asked: "Who is in charge of the clattering train?"

That's the question Daniel asks and answers in his incredible book of stories and prophecies. Intelligent, well-trained, and God-fearing, Daniel was among the first captives taken to Babylon. There he became a powerful statesman in both the Babylonian and Persian empires. His book divides into two parts of six chapters each. The first half tells stories showing the power of God's providence in human affairs. The last half is comprised of visions about the successive kingdoms of earth. Daniel saw the Babylonian kingdom replaced by the Persian, the Persian replaced by the Greek, and the Greek replaced by the Roman—exactly as it later happened in history. But he also saw the eventual establishment of a kingdom that would never be destroyed. His predictions provide a framework for all the rest of biblical prophecy and serve as a backdrop for the book of Revelation. Daniel's overarching message is that the Most High rules over the affairs of men, and God is sovereign over the tides of history.

As we read the headlines each day, we're led to wonder: "Who is in charge of the clattering train?" But when we read Daniel, we know the answer: Heaven rules. The Most High is laying the tracks of history and steering it toward its final destination.

KEY THOUGHT:

The Most High God is sovereign
over the kingdoms of men and over
the tides of human history.

KEY VERSE:

"Those who are wise shall shine like the brightness
of the firmament, and those who turn many to
righteousness like the stars forever and ever."
Daniel 12:3

KEY ACTION:

We must serve God faithfully, resolved
to remain undefiled in a godless society,
living prophetically for the future.

KEY PRAYER:

Lord, may I face future times with confidence,
always remembering the maxim: Heaven rules.

Hosea

nfaithfulness mars many a marriage, and some homes don't survive the trauma; yet God's grace can step into even the hardest spots. In the book of Hosea, we have a poignant story of a prophet married to a prostitute, and of a husband's undying love. The love story between Hosea and his wife Gomer symbolizes God's love for us, even when we fail.

Here's the background: God formed a covenant with Israel that can be likened to a marriage union. But after Solomon's death, the nation of Israel split into a northern kingdom, Israel—and a southern kingdom, Judah. Hosea—the only prophet from the North—preached at a time when lying, bloodshed, oppression, injustice, and prostitution were rampant. To underscore Israel's sins, God commanded Hosea to take a wife, who would violate her marriage commitment—and to love her despite her faults—as a picture of God's unconditional love toward His chosen people. Hosea's book is the story of this troubled marriage, and his sermons or chapters accentuate the enduring love of God.

Many Christians will never be unfaithful in marriage, but we're all sometimes unfaithful to our Lord. We drift from allegiance to Christ and allow other preoccupations and pursuits to replace Him in our affections. "Spiritual adultery"— loving something or someone else more than we love God—is destructive and to be forsaken. As Hosea shows us, God's love is deep, intimate, tender, and protective. In His love we have endless forgiveness and heavenly security.

KEY THOUGHT:

Spiritual adultery occurs when we drift
from our allegiance to God and allow
other preoccupations to replace Him
as the focus of our affection.

KEY VERSES:

"I will betroth you to Me forever;
yes, I will betroth you to Me in righteousness
and justice, in lovingkindness and mercy;
I will betroth you to Me in faithfulness,
and you shall know the LORD."
Hosea 2:19-20

KEY ACTION:

It's time to seek the Lord until He comes
and showers His righteousness on us
(see Hosea 10:12).

KEY PRAYER:

Lord, I want to press on to know
You better, seeking Your presence
and Your great blessings.

JOEL

In these days when we fear a coming global economic apocalypse, it's important to be familiar with the message of Joel, a prophet who dealt with economic calamity and its aftermath. In Joel's day, the monetary devastation was caused by locusts, which could destroy a nation's economy overnight. When swarms of locusts descended on an area, they darkened the sky, sounded like a fleet of helicopters, and consumed every plant in their path. They appeared overnight and were gone the next day, obliterating a year's income and leaving devastation behind.

According to Deuteronomy 28:38, locusts were a mark of God's judgment on sin. So it became Joel's mission to tell people they were experiencing God's judgment. He also said the locusts foreshadowed something yet to come—the Day of the Lord, the culmination of history in which God's final judgment will occur. The plague of locusts was a signpost for the future.

But there's another theme in Joel—restoration. Joel 2:25 says: "So I will restore to you the years that the swarming locust has eaten."

The easiest way to read Joel is in two parts: Chapters 1:1–2:17 describe the locust invasion and the Day of the Lord. The rest of the book describes the mercy of God in restoring Israel and judging her enemies.

If you feel your life has been devastated, read the book of Joel and consider how God can restore the elements of your life. He not only restores; He makes all things new.

KEY THOUGHT:

The locust plague of Joel's day was a divine judgment, foreshadowing the Day of the Lord which will bring destruction to the ungodly but blessings to God's people.

KEY VERSE:

"Rend your heart, and not your garments;
return to the LORD your God, for He *is* gracious
and merciful, slow to anger, and of great kindness;
and He relents from doing harm."
Joel 2:13

KEY ACTION:

Turn back to God from any and every sin,
for He abundantly pardons and
wonderfully restores.

KEY PRAYER:

God, I rejoice in You, for You are faithful.

Amos

When Paul Harvey gave his famous speech, "So God Made a Farmer," at a 1978 convention of the Future Farmers of America, he began: "God said, 'I need someone willing to get up before dawn, milk cows, work all day in the fields, milk cows again, eat supper, and then go to town and stay past midnight at a meeting of the school board.' So God made a farmer."

Well, I have a feeling Amos would have liked that speech. Amos was a farmer—a sheep breeder and fruit grower—from the town of Tekoa in Judah. In the eighth century B.C., when God needed a plainspoken man to deliver His message to Samaria, He chose a farmer—Amos. Amos traveled north and preached during a period of prosperity. Worship was hollow and injustice filled the land, with the rich trampling the rights of the poor. The book of Amos is a collection of sermons condemning the nations—including Judah and Samaria—for the absence of true worship and the presence of true injustice.

The first two chapters of Amos focus on God's judgment on the nations. The next several chapters warn of judgment on Judah and Samaria. The last half of the final chapter is a beautiful promise of hope and restoration.

Amos tells us God despises the exercise of empty religious ritual. Our conduct must always grow from an authentic desire to love others and please Him, and our lives should always produce a true harvest of justice and righteousness.

KEY THOUGHT:

God hates oppression. His justice will roll down like a river, and His righteousness like a mighty stream (see Amos 5:24).

KEY VERSES:

"'The days are coming,' says the LORD,
'when . . . I will bring back the captives of My people
Israel . . . . I will plant them in their land, and no longer
shall they be pulled up from the land I have given
them,' says the LORD your God."
Amos 9:13-15

KEY ACTION:

Our religious practices are worthless unless we
treat others with integrity and compassion.

KEY PRAYER:

Lord, may I love others in the same spirit in which
You love them, unconditionally and full of grace.

OBADIAH

Sibling rivalry is sometimes as innocent as the competition between brothers who are NFL quarterbacks or sisters who are tennis champions. But on other occasions, sibling rivalry can be tragic. Consider the biblical story of Jacob and Esau, twin sons of Isaac. In the womb, they struggled with each other. In life, they fought. In death, their descendants became two nations in perpetual animosity—Israel and Edom.

Saul, David, and Solomon all battled the Edomites, and Edom committed many sins against the Israelites, especially during the Babylonian invasion. They rejoiced when Jerusalem fell, not realizing they, too, would be swept away by Babylon a few years later.

Obadiah's brief prophecy was a bittersweet consolation for Jews who remained in Judah after Babylon had crushed their nation. He apparently wrote his book after the destruction of Jerusalem but before the invasion of Edom. His twenty-one verses fall into two parts: The first fourteen describe God's judgment on Edom for her treachery against Israel; and the remaining verses give a description of the coming day of the Lord when God will judge all nations and establish Israel as the center of His kingdom on earth.

Obadiah tells us that God will deal justly with those who harm His people. But his book is also a subtle reminder of the importance of family loyalty. We should do our best to live in peace with those we love. As Psalm 133 puts it, how good and pleasant it is when brothers live together in unity.

KEY THOUGHT:

Those who are cruel like the proud leaders of Edom will be judged, but the nation of Israel will eventually be restored in triumph.

KEY VERSES:

"The day of the LORD upon all the nations *is* near . . . .
But on Mount Zion there shall be deliverance,
and there shall be holiness."
Obadiah 1:15, 17

KEY ACTION:

When you feel mistreated by others, leave it
with God who sees everything; and rest your case
with Him who deals justly with His people.

KEY PRAYER:

Heavenly Father, give me a love for others that
rejoices when they succeed, not when they fail.

JONAH

Maybe you've heard of Roy Riegels, better known as "Wrong Way Roy." In the 1929 Rose Bowl, he got mixed up and ran sixty-nine yards in the wrong direction. It's been called the worst blunder in college football history. Well, he reminds me of "Wrong Way Jonah," who ran off toward Tarshish when God told him to go to Nineveh. Had Jonah obeyed—taking a message of repentance immediately to the Gentile nation of Assyria—the book that bears his name might read more like those of the other Minor Prophets. Instead, the record of his ministry is an intensely personal story of God's grace to a rebellious prophet, not just to a wicked pagan nation.

Jonah did finally end up going to Nineveh, but he resisted the entire way. And when the Ninevites repented and avoided judgment, Jonah was undone. The book ends with a pouting prophet more concerned for his own comfort than for the multitudes of Assyria.

As God probed Jonah with questions about his values, priorities, and actions, we should answer those questions too. We all arrive at a similar crossroads at some point. When the book of Jonah ends, we see the procrastinating prophet who had still not made up his mind. But his moment of hesitation becomes a moment for each of us: God's call is on our lives right now, and He has a mission for us today. Will we go the wrong way? Or will we go with Him all the way?

KEY THOUGHT:

We must never run away from God's devotion to evangelism, His compassion for souls, or His direction in taking the Gospel to the nations.

KEY VERSE:

"I cried out to the LORD because of
my affliction, and He answered me.
Out of the belly of Sheol I cried,
and You heard my voice."
Jonah 2:2

KEY ACTION:

Go wherever the Lord sends you
without hesitation or vacillation.

KEY PRAYER:

Lord, when my soul faints,
I will remember You and Your
perfect will for my life.

ICAH

According to a British survey, an average citizen of the United Kingdom knowingly violates five rules a week, which amounts to 260 rules a year, or 16,250 in a lifetime. These range from jaywalking to littering to piggybacking on someone else's wireless service. Of course, with millions of laws on the books, it's hard for any of us to make it through a week without some kind of infraction. Micah 6:8 suggests a far simpler code of conduct: "He has shown you, O man, what is good; and what does the LORD require of you but to do justly, to love mercy, and to walk humbly with your God."

It was a needed message in Micah's time. Micah prophesied during the reigns of Jotham, Ahaz, and Hezekiah. These were days of inequality and idolatry. Hezekiah was the best of these kings, but even his reforms had only a temporary effect.

Micah preached about both judgment and hope. Israel's sins could not be overlooked, but neither could the promises of

God—including the prophecy involving the little town of Bethlehem, where a Messiah would be born, a Ruler whose goings forth were from old, even from everlasting.

Sometimes we make the Christian life into something it's not—placing ourselves under arbitrary, self-imposed rules, long lists of do's and don'ts, restrictive disciplines, and complicated objectives. The prophet Micah, however, boils it all down by asking, "What does the LORD require?" He requires us to do justly, love mercy, and walk humbly with Him.

KEY THOUGHT:

Sin devastates; but we have the promise
of a ruler to be born in Bethlehem,
whose goings forth are from old,
even from everlasting.

KEY VERSE:

"He has shown you, O man, what *is* good;
and what does the LORD require of you
but to do justly, to love mercy, and to
walk humbly with your God?"
Micah 6:8

KEY ACTION:

We need to live justly, loving mercy,
and walking humbly with God.

KEY PRAYER:

Dear Lord, teach me Your ways
that I may walk in Your paths.

NAHUM

If you're unfamiliar with Nahum, you will receive a blessing as you study his book. He's one of the most literary of the prophets, employing a wide range of styles and techniques in writing. One of his most memorable verses is Nahum 1:15: "Behold on the mountains the feet of him who brings good tidings, who proclaims peace!"

A word of background will help you better appreciate Nahum. Under the preaching of Jonah, Assyria's capital had repented of her sin and been spared God's judgment. But a newly rebellious generation arose and went back on the warpath against the Israelites. About forty years after Jonah, Assyria invaded Israel. That's when God moved Nahum to announce that Assyria's days were numbered, and to comfort God's people with the assurance that the Lord would bring all nations to justice in His time. Reflecting on tumultuous events, Nahum wrote: "The LORD has His way in the whirlwind and in the storm, and the clouds are the dust of His feet" (1:3).

Nahum's prophecies, which date about 640 B.C., can read with this general outline in mind: Chapter 1: The Lord is the judge of Nineveh. Chapter 2: God's judgment on Nineveh will be swift and violent. Chapter 3: God will utterly destroy Nineveh.

We all face storms in life. Nahum reminds us that God is not absent in the storm. Though the skies grow dark, the wind howls, and the dust flies, God never loses sight of His children. He sees our plight, and He is fully in control.

KEY THOUGHT:

Though nations mock, strut, intimidate,
and terrorize the innocent, one day the world
will reap what it sows; but God's people
have Good news to take to the world.

KEY VERSE:

"Behold, on the mountains the feet of him
who brings good tidings, who proclaims peace!
O Judah, keep your appointed feasts, perform
your vows. For the wicked one shall no more
pass through you; he is utterly cut off."
Nahum 1:15

KEY ACTION:

Though skies are often dark, we must
realize God is not absent from the storm;
and He never loses sight of His children.

KEY PRAYER:

Thank You, God! You are good,
a refuge in times of trouble.

HABAKKUK

Sometimes we don't like the way our world is shaping up. When we watch the news, we're disturbed. When we look around at our own family or finances or failures, we don't like what we see there either. Life can disturb us. That's how Habakkuk felt, and the Lord has given us this book to show us how the prophet worked through his emotions by faith and prayer.

The book of Habakkuk isn't a set of sermons. It's an unusual conversation between Habakkuk and his God about what was happening in Judah. Troubled by the life of the nation, Habakkuk wondered why God would let Judah pursue an ungodly path. The Lord replied, in effect, "Be patient, Habakkuk. I will send Babylon to judge Judah for her sins."

That raised more questions: How could God use a godless nation to judge Judah? The Lord assured Habakkuk that Babylon would face judgment too. By the end of the book,

Habakkuk had a clearer understanding of the heart and hand of God. In response, he composed one of the most beautiful expressions of faith found anywhere in the Bible, one we too can use to express our faith in faltering times: "Though the fig tree may not blossom, nor there be fruit on the vines . . . yet I will rejoice in the LORD, I will joy in the God of my salvation. The LORD God is my strength; He makes my feet like deer's feet; He makes me walk on high places" (Habakkuk 3:17-19).

KEY THOUGHT:

When we don't like the way our world is
shaping up, we're in the best possible place
to learn how the righteous live by faith.

KEY VERSES:

"Though the fig tree may not blossom,
nor fruit be on the vines; though the labor
of the olive may fail, and the fields yield
no food . . . yet I will rejoice in the LORD,
I will joy in the God of my salvation."
Habakkuk 3:17-18

KEY ACTION:

We must live by faith, not by sight,
trusting God fully even when everything
seems to fail around us.

KEY PRAYER:

My Lord and my God, please do something in my life
that is unbelievable, and beyond my capability,
that You may get all the glory and praise!

ZEPHANIAH

Some time ago, a popular book entitled *The Self-Destructive Habits of Good Companies* made the rounds in leadership circles. It warned about complacency—the sense of security deriving from the belief that our past successes will continue indefinitely.

The prophet Zephaniah wrote a similar book to the nation of Judah about the risk of spiritual complacency. He warned, "It shall come to pass at that time that I will search Jerusalem with lamps, and punish the men who are settled in complacency, who say in their heart, 'The Lord will not do good, nor will He do evil'" (Zephaniah 1:12). In Zephaniah's day, complacency had settled over Jerusalem like an invisible fog. People in the once-devout City of David had convinced themselves that the Lord would not intervene, regardless of how they acted. Yet only a generation later, disaster overtook them.

Zephaniah is called the Prophet of the Day of the Lord. He

announced the coming of the day of the Lord against Judah, predicted judgments on five other nations, then consoled God's people with a promise of a future restoration in Jerusalem. His central theme is this imminent day of reckoning for Judah and the nations. But his prophetic warnings also point to a future day of judgment for the entire complacent world.

Always guard against complacency. Ask God to show you where your security truly lies and to move you into the only true shelter in the world—a living relationship with the Lord Jesus Christ.

KEY THOUGHT:

The Day of the Lord will come with
a whirlwind of inevitable destruction
on the complacent and ungodly, but
will also bring the fulfillment of the
ages to God's people.

KEY VERSE:

"The LORD your God in your midst, the
Mighty One, will save; He will rejoice over you
with gladness, He will quiet *you* with His love,
He will rejoice over you with singing."
Zephaniah 3:17

KEY ACTION:

Rejoice in the love of a God
who rejoices over you in song.

KEY PRAYER:

Lord, help me to be meek and humble,
and to trust in Your Name.

HAGGAI

In the ancient world, orators were rock stars. Their rhetoric established cities, changed laws, and started wars. In today's world, motivational speakers occupy the same role, and they get paid big bucks for their words. The best motivational speakers easily command six-figure fees for every speech.

The prophet Haggai was one of the Bible's great motivational speakers. He gave his messages for free, but their value was beyond any price imaginable. Under his ministry, a project that had stalled for sixteen years was resumed and completed. And it wasn't just an ordinary project—it was the rebuilding of the Jewish Temple.

Years after the Babylonian exile, a remnant of Jews returned to Jerusalem to reestablish their city and rebuild the temple of the Lord. The work was hard, the resources sparse, and the opposition great. In great discouragement, the workers suspended the project and began building their own houses.

Then Haggai came with some messages from the Lord, delivered during a four-month period in 520 B.C. He called Israel back to obedience and back to their true priorities, and he motivated them to finish the task of rebuilding God's house.

We often find life is hard, resources sparse, and opposition great. In discouragement, we sometimes reverse our priorities and fail to do what God most wants us to do. We put our comfort ahead of God's cause. Haggai's message is: Consider your ways, cast off discouragement, put first things first, and finish the task assigned to you.

KEY THOUGHT:

The priority of finishing God's work
should come before the priorities of our
own comfort and convenience.

KEY VERSES:

Then the word of the LORD came by Haggai the prophet, saying, 'Is it time for you yourselves to dwell in your paneled houses, and this temple *to lie* in ruins?' Now, therefore, thus says the LORD of hosts: 'Consider your ways!'"
Haggai 1:3-5

KEY ACTION:

Be strong, all you people of the land, and work. For God is with you (see Haggai 2:4).

KEY PRAYER:

Father, give me strength to finish the work You have put before me. Fill me with Your Spirit.

ZECHARIAH

uthor Muriel Anderson credits four words with launching her career as a writer: *Of course you can!* "I was fortunate to have had a father," she said, "who was good at shouting *of course you can* at just the right moments."

That was the message of Zechariah. According to the book of Ezra, the exiles returning to Jerusalem after the captivity began rebuilding the temple, but gave up in discouragement. The project was abandoned for years. Then the post-exilic prophets, Haggai and Zechariah, came preaching, saying, in effect: "Of course you can rebuild this temple." The people of Jerusalem, spurred on by these prophets, resumed and completed the work.

Much of Zechariah's encouragement involved his emphasis on the Messiah. No other Old Testament book gives more information about Christ: His humble appearance and humanity, His rejection and suffering, His betrayal for thirty pieces of silver, His priesthood and kingship, His glorious return to earth, and His ultimate victory and reign.

The first six chapters of Zechariah present visions of God in control of the world. Chapters 7 and 8 deal with the responsibilities of God's people. The last five chapters are a series of prophetic visions of the future and the culmination of God's program in human history.

When it comes to fulfilling the will of God, the message of Zechariah is: "Of course you can." As chapter 4:6 says: "Not by might, nor by power, but by My Spirit, says the LORD of hosts."

KEY THOUGHT:

Rebuilding the post-exilic temple was nothing less than a vital and visual preparatory step for the coming Messiah and the ultimate Day of the Lord.

KEY VERSES:

"This *is* the word of the LORD to Zerubbabel: 'Not by might nor by power, but by My Spirit,' says the LORD of hosts. 'Who *are* you, O great mountain? Before Zerubbabel *you shall become* a plain! And he shall bring forth the capstone with shouts of "'Grace, grace to it!'"'"
Zechariah 4:6-7

KEY ACTION:

Never be discouraged when the work seems small or slow, for God's Spirit uses little events and unknown people in powerful ways.

KEY PRAYER:

Lord, remind me that little is much if You are in it.

MALACHI

All of us benefit from good counseling, whether it's marital counseling, financial counseling, legal counseling, or simply getting advice from a friend. But imagine sitting down and having a counseling session with God Himself. That's the format of the book of Malachi. It's a unique approach in Scripture, as Malachi shares the back-and-forth conversations God wanted to have with His children at the end of the Old Testament.

Malachi appeared on the scene almost a century after Haggai and Zechariah. The spiritual life of Israel had declined in the interval, and Malachi spoke about bored priests, blemished sacrifices, and hard-hearted people who were just going through the motions of worship.

Malachi's prophecy is written in the form of a dialogue between God and the people of Israel, centered on six issues. These six arguments and their subject matter provide a general outline for the book, as Malachi deals with (one) God's love for Israel; (two) the people's careless approach to worship; (three) the nation's careless view of marriage; (four) the injustice that filled the land; (five) the sin of withholding tithes; and (six) God's intention to judge sinners and reward the faithful.

These areas are as relevant to us as to the people of Malachi's day; and as we read his book, we need to put ourselves in the counseling chair and hear the Lord say to us and to our land as He said in Malachi 3:7: "'Return to Me, and I will return to you,' says the Lord of hosts."

KEY THOUGHT:

Spiritual apathy is a dangerous
condition, one we must guard
against with all our hearts.

KEY VERSE:

"'Try Me now in this,' says the LORD of hosts,
'if I will not open for you the windows of heaven
and pour out for you *such* blessing that *there will
not be* room enough *to receive it.*'"
Malachi 3:10

KEY ACTION:

We must return with fervor to the Lord,
to genuine worship, to high moral values,
to marital commitment, and to the practices
of tithing and godly fellowship.

KEY PRAYER:

Lord, may you find me worthy to receive
abundant blessings from Your hand.

BOOKS OF THE
NEW TESTAMENT

MATTHEW

Whenever Jesus passes by, lives are changed. Take, for example, the tax collector Matthew. One day he was sitting in his tax booth when Jesus walked by, looked him in the eye, and said, "Follow Me" (Matthew 9:9). Just that quickly, Matthew "left all, rose up, and followed Him" (Luke 5:29).

Matthew later wrote the first Gospel, an account of the words and works of Jesus penned for his fellow Jews, probably between A.D. 50 and 60. The Gospel of Matthew had one overriding purpose: to demonstrate that the carpenter from Nazareth was the long-awaited Messiah—Christ, the Anointed One. Matthew packed his Gospel with Old Testament links, quoting and alluding to the Old Testament more than any other New Testament writer. His Gospel is wholly cut from Jewish cloth. Yet it's a garment for Jews and Gentiles alike. Matthew began his book with the visit of the Gentile Magi at the birth of Christ, and concluded his Gospel with the commission to make disciples of all nations.

Matthew, which is structured around five major discourses of Jesus, emphasizes the kingdom of heaven, our Lord's role as Messiah, the fulfillment of Old Testament prophecies, and the worldwide nature of the Gospel. As the Promised One, Jesus is worthy of our hope. As Messiah, He is worthy of our trust. As King, He is worthy of our devotion. As Savior, His name should be proclaimed to all the earth, and, lo, He is with us, even to the end of the age.

KEY THOUGHT:

Jesus Christ, Son of David,
Son of Abraham, is the Messiah,
the King of Israel, the Savior
of the world.

KEY VERSES:

"He asked His disciples, saying, 'Who do men say that I, the Son of Man, am?' . . . Simon Peter answered and said, 'You are the Christ, the Son of the living God.'"
Matthew 16:13, 16

KEY ACTION:

Make disciples of all the nations, baptizing them in the name of the Father, of the Son, and of the Holy Spirit (see Matthew 28:19-20).

KEY PRAYER:

May my life reflect the glory of Your name.

MARK

Κατὰ Μᾶρκον

A business leader recently wrote a book about urgency, because, he said, most people are complacent and don't realize it. If anything is going to happen for the better, he wrote, it must be tackled with urgency.

That's a good way to describe the Gospel of Mark. This book is short and to the point—an approach reflecting the attitude of Rome's culture. The Roman world of Mark's day was focused on getting things done—*now*! So Mark used words like *immediately* and *quickly* almost fifty times to describe the urgency and immediacy of Jesus' mission and message.

Mark had been a teenager in Jerusalem during the ministry of Christ. He was caught up in the events of our Lord's death and resurrection; and his mother's home was probably the location of the Upper Room where Jesus met with His disciples and, later, where the Holy Spirit descended at Pentecost.

As a young man, Mark faltered on Paul's first missionary journey, but he later became a respected leader and, according to tradition, a close associate of Simon Peter. His Gospel likely reflects Peter's action-packed record of Christ's life.

Mark wrote his Gospel during a time when everything dear was being swept away by marching armies, mindless persecution, injustice, and death. His Gospel helped the Roman world focus like a laser on the story of Jesus. So it is today. The more chaotic our world, the more urgently we must proclaim the Gospel of Jesus Christ, the Son of God.

KEY THOUGHT:

The Son of God had supreme power,
which He used to serve others with urgency
and to sacrifice His life for the world.

KEY VERSES:

"Whoever desires to become great
among you shall be your servant . . .
For even the Son of Man did not
come to be served, but to serve, and
to give His life a ransom for many."
Mark 10:43, 45

KEY ACTION:

When we become disciples of Jesus Christ,
we're seized with urgency as we serve others
and share His Good News with a needy world.

KEY PRAYER:

Lord, may I be a servant of all
and thereby glorify Your name!

LUKE

Have you ever lost a wallet or a purse? Or far worse, perhaps you've had a moment when you turned around and realized your child had wandered off in a crowd. It's an awful feeling to know someone or something is lost.

Luke, the Bible's only Gentile author, was gripped by the needs of lost people. As we read his Gospel, we notice how he emphasized stories of the poor and downtrodden. Luke was a physician, sensitive to the needs of those who crossed his path. As he tells the story of Christ, the humanity of Jesus is revealed— we see how our Lord made salvation available to people on the margins of society, like needy widows, obscure shepherds, despised tax collectors, and troubled children. In chapter 15, Luke tells of three people who lost things very precious to them, and each story ends with the joy of reclamation. In Luke 19:10, he drove home his theme, saying: "For the Son of Man has come to seek and to save that which was lost."

Luke wrote with passion and conviction, but his Gospel isn't emotionally-driven; it's factually-based. In his opening paragraph, Luke prefaced his book by calling it an orderly account, well investigated, setting forth the certainty of the facts related to the life of Christ. From a literary perspective, Luke's writing stands out within ancient literature. From a faith perspective, his accuracy provides well-researched reasons to believe in Jesus, the one who came to seek and to save those who are lost.

KEY THOUGHT:

Jesus Christ is Savior for the entire world,
for everyone, Jew and Gentile alike,
for all are lost and need to be saved.

KEY VERSE:

"For the Son of Man has come to seek
and to save that which was lost."
Luke 19:10

KEY ACTION:

The followers of Christ must be gripped
by the needs of lost people, seek them
with the message of life, and rejoice
with the angels when they come to Christ.

KEY PRAYER:

Lord, thank you for saving me
and redeeming my soul.

JOHN

We have many friends, but only one or two are *best* friends—those who are very special to us, whom we call even when we have nothing much to talk about. An acronym has seeped into our society to describe these special people: BFF—Best Friends Forever.

Without being irreverent we can think of the apostle John as our Lord's best friend. Among His twelve disciples, Jesus chose three to be with Him at critical moments: Peter, James, and John. Within that circle, John seemed to have a special relationship with Jesus. Five times in his Gospel he described himself as "the disciple whom Jesus loved."

Matthew, Mark, and Luke take a biographical approach to Jesus' life. John is more thematic and theological. He loved to show patterns in the Lord's ministry, such as the seven signs Jesus performed and His seven "I am" statements. The subject of "life" is a primary theme in John—eternal life, abundant life, the bread of life, the water of life; and the way, the truth, and the life. John's goal was to portray Christ as God who became flesh to save those who believe in Him. "These [things] are written," he said, "that you may believe that Jesus is the Christ, the Son of God, and that believing you may have life in His name" (John 20:31).

We too can be disciples whom Jesus loves. If you're lonely, study John, discover Jesus' abundant life, and realize that by grace He is your best friend forever.

KEY THOUGHT:

Jesus Christ, the Son of God, is the Word—God
Himself—who became flesh, dwelled among us,
and gave Himself for us, that all who believe in Him
"should not perish but have everlasting life."

KEY VERSE:

"But these are written that you may believe
that Jesus is the Christ, the Son of God, and that
believing you may have life in His name."
John 20:31

KEY ACTION:

"You must be born again" (see John 3:7).

KEY PRAYER:

God, thank you for sending Your Son,
Jesus Christ, to die for my sins.

Acts

What exciting days to be followers of Christ! The Church around the world is growing faster than ever, and the number of Christians is exploding. Some people say we're living in the twenty-ninth chapter of the book of Acts. Well, in a sense these last 2000 years of Christian history have been a continuation of the story that began in the twenty-eight chapters of Acts.

In our English Bibles, the fifth book of the New Testament is commonly called, "The Acts of the Apostles." In some ways that title seems a bit misleading. Only two apostles are prominently featured in Acts—Peter and Paul. And the acts that unfold are really the Acts of the Holy Spirit, or, as some said, "The Continuing Words and Works of Jesus by His Spirit Through the Apostles."

The author is Luke, the beloved physician who composed the third Gospel. The books of Luke and Acts are twin volumes of a two-part work. Both cover periods of about thirty years. The Gospel starts with the birth of Christ and finishes the story in Jerusalem. The book of Acts starts with the birth of the Church and finishes the story in Rome.

In Acts 17:6, Luke describes the heroes of Acts as "These who have turned the world upside down." If the world ever needed to be turned upside down, it's now. God grant that you too may turn the world upside down, and that we may indeed be living in the twenty-ninth chapter of Acts.

KEY THOUGHT:

Jesus returned to heaven at the end of His earthly ministry, leaving His Spirit-filled followers with the glorious task of taking His message to the ends of the earth.

KEY VERSE:

"You shall receive power when the Holy Spirit has
come upon you; and you shall be witnesses to
Me in Jerusalem, and in all Judea and Samaria,
and to the end of the earth."
Acts 1:8

KEY ACTION:

"We cannot but speak the things
which we have seen and heard."
Acts 4:20

KEY PRAYER:

Lord, give me the power to
reach the world with the Gospel.

ROMANS

M any church-goers today don't want much doctrine to seep into their thinking. They want nice stories, uplifting platitudes, and fluffy comments on favorite verses. Well, they'd better not open the book of Romans! In the sixteen chapters of this epistle, the apostle Paul sets forth the core theology of Christianity. This is the first great doctrinal book in the New Testament, and a first-century course in biblical doctrine. It's a vital follow-up to the historical facts in the Gospels.

In its broad outline, Romans is easy to follow. Its first eleven chapters explain how God justifies us or makes us righteous through Christ. Working our way through these chapters, we see how humanity is corrupted beyond human remedy, how God makes us righteous through Christ, how we have freedom from the power of sin through the Holy Spirit, and how God offers the blessings of righteousness to Gentiles by grafting us into the living promises given to Israel.

The word "therefore" in chapter 12, verse 1, serves as the transition to the last part of Romans, which talks about our duty to live righteously: "I beseech you therefore, brethren, by the mercies of God, that you present your bodies a living sacrifice, holy, acceptable to God." These final chapters are as practical as any portion of Scripture, giving us instructions for Christ-like living.

I love Romans, and I think you will too. It explains our doctrine and our duty as those who are justified by grace through faith in our Lord Jesus.

KEY THOUGHT:

Because we could not become righteous by our own efforts, God provided justification for us by grace through faith in Jesus Christ.

KEY VERSE:

"For if by the one man's offense death reigned through the one, much more those who receive abundance of grace and of the gift of righteousness will reign in life through the One, Jesus Christ."
Romans 5:17

KEY ACTION:

We must receive the abundance of God's grace, which saves us and enables us to reign in life through Christ Jesus.

KEY PRAYER:

Father, I am thankful that nothing can separate me from Your love!

I CORINTHIANS

If you officiate or attend weddings—as I do—you often hear 1 Corinthians 13 being read. It's the love chapter of the Bible, which begins: "Though I speak with the tongues of men and of angels, but have not love, I have become sounding brass or a clanging cymbal."

Perhaps in addressing the Corinthians Paul was speaking to himself, for he needed all the love he could muster in dealing with this dysfunctional church. Corinth was a prominent city in Greece. It was a rich, immoral place, a city without self-control. In the first century, if you talked about "living like a Corinthian," everyone knew what you meant. It was code language for indulging in a wild and unrestrained lifestyle. Paul was concerned that believers in that city were living more like Corinthians than Christians. Both of his letters to Corinth—1 and 2 Corinthians—were problem-solving letters, and 1 Corinthians deals primarily with interchurch problems. As Paul worked his way through the letter, he tackled one troublesome area after another: disunity, immorality, lawsuits, confusion about marriage, abuses of the Lord's Supper, disrespect in worship, heresy about the Resurrection, and lack of discipline in finances.

But in the middle of it all, he spoke of the love we need for dealing with troublesome people in our lives, and his words still ring true in our hearts: "Love suffers long and is kind; love . . . bears all things, believes all things, hopes all things, endures all things. Love never fails" (1 Corinthians 13:4, 7-8).

KEY THOUGHT:

Christians are to live more like citizens of heaven than citizens of earth, which requires us to exhibit healthy hearts and united churches.

KEY VERSES:

"My speech and my preaching were not with persuasive words of human wisdom, but in demonstration of the Spirit and of power, that your faith should not be in the wisdom of men but in the power of God."
1 Corinthians 2:4-5

KEY ACTION:

Ask the Lord of the Church to restore the selfless love that only He can give and grow.

KEY PRAYER:

God, please give me the "agape" love that never fails.

II CORINTHIANS

If you find yourself slandered in today's world, there are many ways to set the record straight, for we have access to modern communication and technology. But in the first century, the apostle Paul didn't have modern media. It was difficult for him to defend himself. Second Corinthians was essentially a document to prepare the church in Corinth for an imminent visit in which Paul intended to set the record straight about his integrity and authority.

Paul had founded the church in Corinth on his second missionary journey. But after his departure, false apostles had arrived. Their hurtful slander infected the believers. These false apostles, Paul declared in 2 Corinthians, were agents of Satan masquerading as ministers of righteousness. Paul described his own sufferings for Christ and appealed to the Corinthians to remember that "You are our epistle," he said, "written in our hearts, known and read by all men" (2 Corinthians 3:2).

It's not necessary to answer all our critics or to defend ourselves for the sake of pride or legacy. But when an attack harms the cause of Christ, that's different. How wonderful to be able to say, as Paul did 2 Corinthians 5:20-21: "Now then, we are ambassadors for Christ, as though God were pleading through us: we implore you on Christ's behalf, be reconciled to God. For He made Him who knew no sin to be sin for us, that we might become the righteousness of God in Him."

KEY THOUGHT:

Those who represent Christ must have a clear message and godly motives and methods, so that their integrity will be obvious even amid slander.

KEY VERSES:

"Now then, we are ambassadors for Christ, as though God were pleading through us: we implore you on Christ's behalf, be reconciled to God. For He made Him who knew no sin to be sin for us, that we might become the righteousness of God in Him."
2 Corinthians 5:20-21

KEY ACTION:

Slander in the work of Christ is temporary; service for the cause of Christ is eternal.

KEY PRAYER:

Lord, I am righteous only because of Your righteousness.

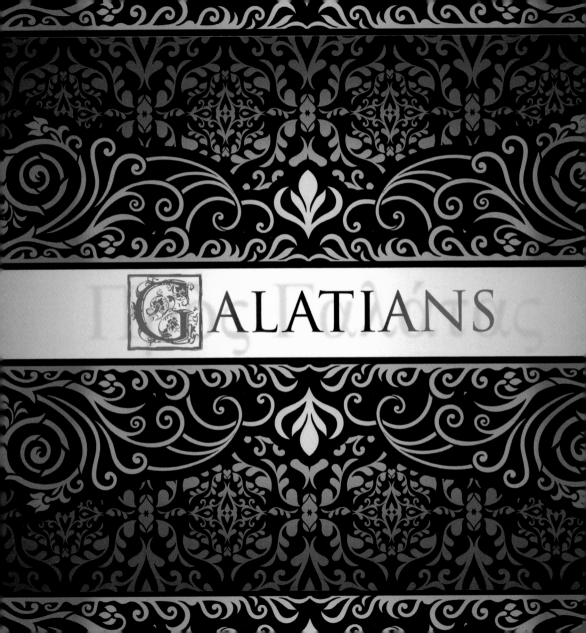

GALATIANS

Some Christians attend liberal churches, and some are in congregations marked by legalism. It's important for us to be sound in our faith, with the right balances and a strong grip on the theology of grace. That's where the book of Galatians comes in.

During the early days of the church, the first Christians were almost all Jews, and many thought Christianity was simply Judaism plus Christ. To become a Christian, one had to first become a Jew, then add Jesus to the equation. But the apostle Paul taught that pagans could come directly to Jesus for salvation without first becoming Jews, and this set the stage for a major conflict of the New Testament church. It's likely that Galatians was written sometime around A.D. 48, just before the Jerusalem Council discussed the issue, and following Paul's first missionary journey.

The letter to the Galatians has three parts. First, in chapters

1 and 2, Paul validated his own authority and the process by which he learned the Gospel message. Second, in chapters three and four, he showed how the Old Testament taught the doctrine of justification by faith, using Abraham as a prime example. Finally, in chapters 5 and 6, Paul described the Spirit-led lifestyle of those justified by grace.

We don't have to obey lists or perform deeds to be saved. Our salvation is found in Christ, plus nothing. Faith in Christ alone leads to freedom and produces life-giving spiritual fruit in our lives by which we can bless others.

KEY THOUGHT:

Since we are justified by faith alone and not
by keeping the Law, Christianity is a living
relationship with Christ, not a religion or a ritual.

KEY VERSE:

"We have believed in Christ Jesus, that we
might be justified by faith in Christ
and not by the works of the law."
Galatians 2:16

KEY ACTION:

"Walk in the Spirit, and you shall
not fulfill the lust of the flesh."
Galatians 5:16

KEY PRAYER:

Lord, because I have been "crucified with Christ; it is
no longer I who live, but Christ who lives in me." Thank
you that the life I now live in the flesh, I live by faith in
the One who loved me and gave Himself for me.

EPHESIANS

From year to year, depending on the ebb and flow of the global economy, several people vie for the title: The Richest Person in the World. These people—multi-billionaires—have more money than they can spend, for the earnings and interest on their fortunes exceed all possible expenditure. Yet the richest person on earth is only one heartbeat away from losing everything.

If you want to know who is really the richest on earth, read the book of Ephesians. This Pauline letter catalogues the endless wealth and wondrous riches of God's people. Ephesians tells us about the riches of God's grace, the riches of the glory of His inheritance in the saints, His rich mercy, and of our unsearchable riches in Christ.

Ephesians divides into two parts. The first three chapters stress doctrinal truths, and the last three explain how we should live because of those truths. In other words, chapters 1 through

3 explain why we're rich; and chapters 4 through 6 describe how rich people live—the lifestyle of those who are spiritually wealthy. This includes appreciating the value and unity of His body, the Church.

Because Paul intended Ephesians to circulate among neighboring churches, everything in the book applies to Christians in any place or time, including you and me. From the first words of Ephesians, Paul details the spiritual blessings of every Christian. The entire epistle records the blessings we have in heavenly places, and the incredible difference those blessings make in our lives each day.

KEY THOUGHT:

The riches of God's grace provide an eternal inheritance for His children, an endless wealth of blessings, compelling them to live a life worthy of the calling they have received.

KEY VERSES:

"For by grace you have been saved through faith, and
that not of yourselves; it is the gift of God,
not of works, lest anyone should boast."
Ephesians 2:8-9

KEY ACTION:

Walk in love and be filled with the Spirit
(see Ephesians 5:2, 18).

KEY PRAYER:

Lord, may I walk in love and be filled
with the Spirit so that my life will be
a shining testament to You.

PHILIPPIANS

No church in the New Testament had a more dramatic beginning than the one in Philippi, as described in Acts 16. It involved a businesswoman, a fortuneteller, floggings, singing, and a midnight earthquake. In the midst of these events, Paul planted the Philippian church and watered it with his blood.

Years later during his first Roman imprisonment, Paul wrote this very personal letter to the church. They had a unique place in his heart. In these four chapters, Paul used the words *I, me,* and *my* over one hundred times as he expressed his love and gratitude for the faithful support of this beloved congregation.

It's no wonder, then, that contentment and joy are dominant themes of this letter, along with the Christ-like practice of humble service. In chapter 2, we have one of the most important passages about Christ in the Bible: "who being in the form of God, did not consider it robbery to be equal with God, but made

Himself of no reputation, taking the form of a bondservant" (Philippians 2:6-7). Therefore, said Paul, "God has highly exalted Him and given Him a name above every name that at the name of Jesus every knee shall bow" (Philippians 2:9-10).

In keeping with His example, we too, then, should not look to our own interests but to the interests of others.

Joy, contentment, and humble service! As we internalize Philippians, we'll increasingly share these qualities exhibited by those who confess Jesus Christ as Lord, to the glory of God the Father.

KEY THOUGHT:

Despite persecution and problems, we can rejoice in
the Lord always, not through selfish ambition, but
through Him who strengthens us.

KEY VERSES:

"Therefore, my beloved and longed-for brethren, my joy and crown, so stand fast in the Lord, beloved . . . Rejoice in the Lord always. Again I will say, rejoice!"
Philippians 4:1, 4

KEY ACTION:

"Let this mind be in you which was also in Christ Jesus."
Philippians 2:5

KEY PRAYER:

God, grant me joy, contentment, and peace, regardless of my circumstances.

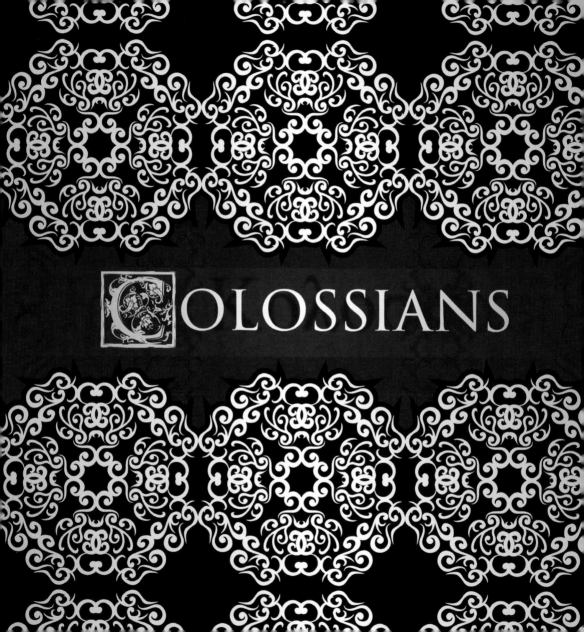

COLOSSIANS

The U.S. Secret Service has a website telling us how to detect counterfeit money before we're swindled. The key is knowing the qualities of genuine bills—the lifelike nature of the portrait, the distinctive depiction of the seal, the fine lines of the border, the singular style of the serial numbers, and the tiny fibers embedded in the paper. By knowing the genuine article, we can spot forgeries.

In the same way, we detect heresy by knowing true biblical doctrine. That's the approach Paul took in this little letter of four chapters.

A man named Epaphras had planted the Colossian church during Paul's prolonged ministry in Ephesus. Some years later, Epaphras grew distressed when error crept into the church. By then Paul was imprisoned in Rome, so Epaphras visited him to share his heartache. In response, Paul wrote this letter in which he went on theological offense, describing Jesus Christ in all His glory, declaring that Christ is the image of the invisible God. Paul proclaimed that Christ alone is enough. No other person, knowledge, or system is needed.

The first two chapters of Colossians are theological in nature; the last two are practical, telling us how to live out the truth of Christ in daily life by the power of the Holy Spirit. The right truth leads to the right testimony. Correct doctrine leads to a winning walk. The more we focus on Jesus, the more our hearts overflow with the reality that in all things He must have the preeminence.

KEY THOUGHT:

Jesus Christ is Lord of all, sufficient
for all our needs and worthy of all
our worship and obedience.

KEY VERSES:

"He is the image of the invisible God,
the firstborn over all creation . . .
the head of the body, the church . . .
the firstborn from the dead, that in
all things He may have the preeminence."
Colossians 1:15, 18

KEY ACTION:

Since we've been raised with Christ,
we must set our hearts on things above,
where Christ reigns (see Colossians 3:1).

KEY PRAYER:

Lord, You are all I need.

I THESSALONIANS

What if no one had a copy of a New Testament in your congregation nor had even heard of one? That was a problem in the early Church. When Paul evangelized the Macedonian city of Thessalonica, for example, few if any New Testament writings were available. When we face questions or problems today, we open our New Testaments; but the young Christians in Thessalonica didn't yet have this inspired resource. That's why Paul wrote to them, and in doing so he contributed one of our favorite books of the New Testament.

The Thessalonians were especially confused about the timing of the Lord's return. When Paul had been among them, he had taught about the Second Coming. But persecution had driven him out of town before he could say all he wanted. From a subsequent report, Paul learned that the church was confused: Has Christ already returned? Could He return in our lifetime? What about our loved ones who have died believing in Christ? Will we see them again?

In 1 Thessalonians (and again in 2 Thessalonians), Paul addressed those questions and outlined the events connected with the Rapture of the Church. He exhorts us to persevere with holiness and expectancy as we await His coming. Since we don't know the precise moment of the Lord's return, it could be *any* moment. As those who belong to Christ, we should watch for His coming; and while waiting, we should live faithfully, righteously, and productively for His glory.

KEY THOUGHT:

Christ is coming quickly!

KEY VERSE:

"Now may the God of peace Himself
sanctify you completely; and may your whole
spirit, soul, and body be preserved blameless
at the coming of our Lord Jesus Christ."
1 Thessalonians 5:23

KEY ACTION:

Since Christ may come at any moment,
we should live productively, faithfully,
and expectantly.

KEY PRAYER:

Lord, though I do not know the day
of Your return, I will live as if today
were the day.

II THESSALONIANS

Those who travel for a living know the burden of long-distance parenting. Thanks to modern technology, we can still read to our kids or talk to them at bedtime. But it's hard to be away from our children when they need us.

That's how Paul felt about the church of the Thessalonians. In Acts 17, he had arrived in this city with the Gospel, but persecution had driven him away before he had adequately instructed his converts. In 1 and 2 Thessalonians, Paul was providing long-distance parenting to his children in the faith.

Both these letters focus on the return of Christ and on the way we ought to live while anticipating that day. In 1 Thessalonians, Paul answered some questions about the Second Coming. But afterward some unknown person, apparently pretending to be Paul, had written that the return of Christ had already occurred. The Thessalonians were understandably confused, so Paul wrote 2 Thessalonians to clear up the issue.

The first chapter of this letter expresses Paul's thanksgiving and prayer for the church. Chapter 2 deals with the events leading up to the Day of the Lord. The last chapter commands us to be busy and productive as we await His coming. Paul's teaching on the End Times should motivate us to be hopeful toward the future and diligent in the present. The purpose of the teaching about the coming of Christ is not for our speculation but for our sanctification as we grow up in Christ.

KEY THOUGHT:

The return of Christ is a future event
that will be swift, certain, and glorious.

KEY VERSES:

"Now may our Lord Jesus Christ Himself, and our God and Father, who has loved us and given us everlasting consolation and good hope by grace, comfort your hearts and establish you in every good word and work."
2 Thessalonians 2:16-17

KEY ACTION:

The Second Coming shouldn't provoke idleness among believers, but action; not speculation, but sanctification.

KEY PRAYER:

God, help me see through the distraction of this world to the glory of Heaven beyond.

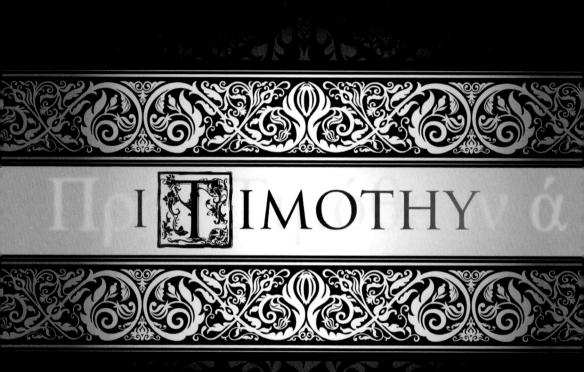

ΤΙΜΌΤΗΥ

Most everything we buy comes with an owner's manual, but if you're like me, looking at those instructions is a last resort. We put it off as long as possible.

Well, the book of 1 Timothy is an instruction manual for the local church. We should read it often and heed it diligently. It's the first of three Pastoral Epistles, as we call them, written between A.D. 62 and 67; and it's addressed to Timothy, a young man we first meet in Acts 16, when he decided to join Paul in his travels. The two become close, and Paul called him, "My true son in the faith" (1 Timothy 1:2).

Years later Timothy was placed in charge of the work in the city of Ephesus. That's when Paul wrote this letter, telling him how to manage certain problems he faced in the ministry—how to confront false teachers, how to order the church's worship, how to select leaders, and how to conduct himself in difficult situations.

The apostle tells us to stand up for the truth in public and to guard our own souls in private. He stressed the themes of doctrinal purity, worship, godliness, leadership, pastoral care, and contentment.

Church work isn't for the faint of heart, and the ministry can often be discouraging. But it always helps to read the manual. In 1 Timothy, the Lord tells us how to conduct ourselves in His house, which is the Church of the living God, the pillar and foundation of the truth.

KEY THOUGHT:

God's Church should be led with excellence by leaders who possess wisdom and integrity.

KEY VERSE:

"Fight the good fight of faith, lay hold on eternal life, to which you were also called and have confessed the good confession in the presence of many witnesses."
1 Timothy 6:12

KEY ACTION:

We must conduct ourselves wisely in the house of God, "which is the church of the living God, the pillar and ground of the truth" (see 1 Timothy 4:15).

KEY PRAYER:

Heavenly Father, I pray for the leaders of my nation and for all in authority over me, that we may lead quiet and peaceable lives in all godliness and reverence.

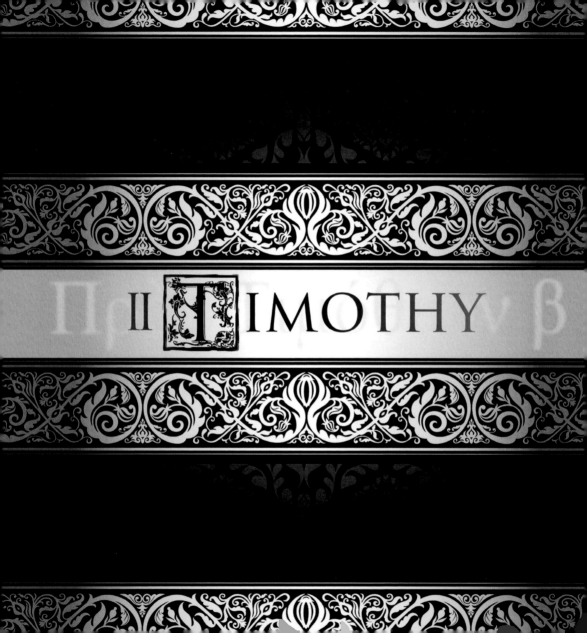

II TIMOTHY

If you read the last words of dying people, you'll find sayings both preposterous and profound. Playwright Oscar Wilde, for example, said as he died in a drab hotel: "Either that wallpaper goes, or I do."

Well, there was no drivel from Paul's pen as he recorded his last words in 2 Timothy. Confined to Rome's Mamertine Prison, Paul told Timothy: "The time of my departure is at hand. I have fought the good fight, I have finished the race, I have kept the faith . . . Be diligent to come quickly . . . to come before winter" (2 Timothy 4:7, 9, 21).

Many of Paul's companions had abandoned or turned against him. He needed Timothy's help—as well as a coat and some books—while awaiting execution. So as we read 2 Timothy, we feel we're reading a final letter from a father to his son, giving us Paul's last testimony and final instructions.

Second Timothy emphasizes faithfulness. Paul spoke of his own faithfulness and exhorted Timothy to be faithful to his calling and gifts, particularly to preaching the Word. He tells us to persevere like a soldier in the army, an athlete in the games, or a farmer in the fields.

None of us knows if we'll have the opportunity for last words. But we can live a life of faithfulness now, leaving a legacy for those who follow, as we fight the good fight and keep the faith, looking forward to the crown of righteousness, which the Lord, the righteous Judge, will give us on that day.

KEY THOUGHT:

In perilous times, we must be steadfast
and determined to fight the good fight,
finish the race, and keep the faith.

KEY VERSES:

"God has not given us a spirit of fear,
but of power and of love and of a sound mind.
Therefore do not be ashamed of the testimony
of our Lord, nor of me His prisoner, but share
with me in the sufferings for the gospel."
2 Timothy 1:7-8

KEY ACTION:

"The things that you have heard from
me among many witnesses, commit
these to faithful men who will be
able to teach others also."
2 Timothy 2:2

KEY PRAYER:

Lord, You are faithful. In good times,
and bad. You are faithful.

A construction company in Belize recently destroyed one of the nation's largest Mayan pyramids while excavating for a new road. The loss is incalculable, and authorities blame it on laziness. Builders were too slothful to figure a way around the treasure, so they took the easy way out—bulldozing through it without thinking.

We do a lot of damage by taking the easy way out. In the book of Titus, the apostle Paul told his troubleshooter, Titus, how to minister to people who were converted from a culture filled with "liars, evil beasts, and lazy gluttons" (Titus 1:12). The setting was the island of Crete, which Paul and Titus had evangelized. Titus remained on the island to get the churches organized and to develop the work. But he struggled to oversee churches filled with people who had grown up without self-discipline.

That sounds like a relevant subject, doesn't it? How do we move from laziness to self-control and spiritual maturity? In chapter

1, Paul laid down the qualifications of mature and hard-working church leaders. In chapters 2 and 3, he told Titus what to say to various groups and to the Church as a whole.

The same grace that brought salvation, he wrote, teaches us to say "No" to worldly passions, to deny laziness and lust, and to live soberly and righteously in this world. The message of Titus is: God's work should be well-organized and His workers self-controlled as we go about building—not bulldozing—His Church in this world.

KEY THOUGHT:

Godly leaders should set in order what is lacking
in the Church by teaching sound doctrine
and modeling self-discipline.

KEY VERSES:

"Denying ungodliness and worldly lusts,
we should live soberly, righteously, and godly in the
present age, looking for the blessed hope and glorious
appearing of our great God and Savior Jesus Christ."
Titus 2:12-13

KEY ACTION:

"Speak the things which are proper
for sound doctrine . . . Be careful
to maintain good works."
Titus 2:1 and 3:8

KEY PRAYER:

Dear God, help me seek sound doctrine,
and create a strong desire within me to
be nourished by Your Word.

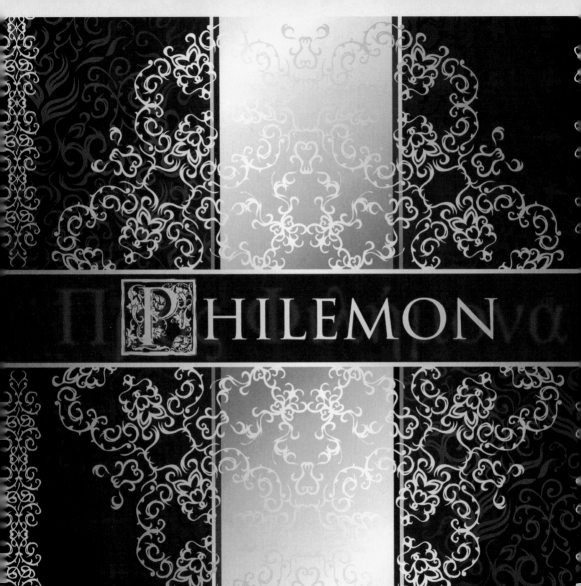

PHILEMON

There are two things we seldom see nowadays—a personal handwritten note; and someone who says to us, "Put that on my bill."

In this little letter, a man named Philemon received both.

This is one of the most personal stories in the Bible, and it provides us with Paul's only piece of truly private correspondence in Scripture. Paul wrote it from prison, addressed to a wealthy man named Philemon who lived in the Turkish town of Colosse.

Philemon possessed bondservants, one of whom—Onesimus—had run away and fled to Rome. It's likely he had robbed Philemon. There in the capital city of Rome, Onesimus crossed paths with the apostle Paul who led him to faith in Christ. The young man found new life, and Paul took this boy into his heart like a father to his son, mentoring and discipling him. But the day came for Onesimus to be sent back to Philemon with this slip of a letter, an appeal from Paul to Philemon regarding Onesimus. "Receive this young man as a brother," said Paul, and "if he has wronged you or owes anything, put that on my account" (Philemon 1:17-18).

Onesimus left a runaway slave; he returned a dear brother, and we're left with a book that teaches us the power of forgiveness and reconciliation. We can't claim to experience God's love if we refuse to forgive others. Christian forgiveness knows no boundaries. Christ put our sins on His account that we might be both forgiven and forgiving.

KEY THOUGHT:

Being members of God's family obligates us
to attitudes of forgiveness, reconciliation, and
mutual respect, one for another.

KEY VERSES:

"I appeal to you for my son Onesimus, whom I have begotten while in my chains, who once was unprofitable to you, but now is profitable to you and to me."
Philemon 1:10-11

KEY ACTION:

Receive, respect, and refresh your brothers and sisters in Christ.

KEY PRAYER:

Lord, may the sharing of my faith become effective by the acknowledgement of every good thing I have in Christ.

EBREWS

The president of a Christian university was famous for telling discouraged students: "It's always too soon to quit." Those words ring true for all of us, because life is difficult and we sometimes want to give up. Hebrews was written to tell us to persevere, to keep going, to focus on our great high priest, and to run with patience the race before us.

According to background given in chapter 10, Hebrews was addressed to some Jewish Christians facing renewed challenges. Though they had confessed Christ as Savior and been faithful in the past, they now faced a new wave of persecution. Some were in danger of reverting to Judaism.

The writer of Hebrews—whoever he was—exhorted them to remain strong in Him who is greater than anything or anyone in the Old Testament. Jesus is truly our great High Priest, who instituted a new and better covenant and who ever lives to make intercession for His people. Words like *better, more, great,* and *greater* appear about forty-five times in this book, making Hebrews a book of superlatives about Jesus, who is superior to all the angels, prophets, writers, systems and sacrifices of Old Testament days.

While most of us don't have a heritage steeped in Levitical tradition, we all face discouragement. Hebrews tells us to hold firm to our faith, keeping our eyes on our Great High Priest, and to persevere, never giving up. With Christ on our side, it's always too soon to quit.

KEY THOUGHT:

We must never yield to discouragement,
for our Great High Priest is supreme
over all and sufficient for all.

KEY VERSE:

"Seeing then that we have a great High Priest who has passed through the heavens, Jesus the Son of God, let us hold fast our confession."
Hebrews 4:14

KEY ACTION:

Persevere!

KEY PRAYER:

Lord, help me finish the race You have put before me! Give me strength to be a champion of the faith.

JAMES

Most of us know the value of a wise pastor to whom we can go for advice and counsel, someone whose biblical messages give us daily nourishment and practical guidance, who cares for us and speaks wisdom to our circumstances.

Well, all of us have a pastor like that whenever we read the book of James.

As the half-brother of the Lord Jesus, James was a respected leader in the early Church; and he became the head of the church in Jerusalem. In that role he wrote these five chapters to fellow Jewish Christians outside Jerusalem, to those scattered abroad. James spoke to them as though he were their pastor, giving commands, warnings, wisdom, and instruction.

As we study this epistle, we become equal recipients of its message. In some ways, the book of James resembles Proverbs. It's pithy, practical, and full of everyday wisdom, and it's advice we need. "The wisdom that is from above," James said, "is first pure, then peaceable, gentle, willing to yield, full of mercy and good fruits, without partiality and without hypocrisy" (James 3:17). True faith, he wrote, is wise and translates into daily action.

If you need a regular dose of wisdom from a beloved pastor, read the book of James and listen to his instructions about dealing with trials, caring for widows and orphans, taming your tongue, and managing your money. The more we know of this little letter, the more the wisdom of our ways and the integrity of our walk will increase.

KEY THOUGHT:

The wisdom from above—God's wisdom—teaches
us how to deal with trials, care for the needy,
control our temper and tongues, and glorify God
by the integrity of our daily lives.

KEY VERSE:

"But be doers of the word, and not
hearers only, deceiving yourselves."
James 1:22

KEY ACTION:

"Pure and undefiled religion before God and the Father
is this: to visit orphans and widows in their trouble,
and to keep oneself unspotted from the world."
James 1:27

KEY PRAYER:

Lord, I ask You for wisdom and
integrity, and the grace with which
to demonstrate it.

I PETER

I f someone had the capacity to retain everything he read, of remembering every fact and date, of summoning to mind every particle of learning; if he could tell you the answer to every question on every exam and provide every statistic known to man—he still would have nothing valuable to say without one other component—experience.

That's why we read 1 Peter with such interest. Simon Peter was one of our Lord's original followers and he experienced every dimension of discipleship, both good and bad. He'd been on the mountaintop with Christ, had walked to Him on the water, had fled from Him at the cross, and had served Him in the early Church. In 1 Peter, the old fisherman drew from a lifetime of experience to tell us how to conduct ourselves as pilgrims and strangers in the world.

Peter hit several themes in his letter, including our conduct, the power of grace, the importance of submission and separation, and the role of tribulation in life. Much of his letter is written with suffering in mind, teaching us how to respond when grieved by various trails. We're to commit ourselves to God, to follow in the footsteps of Christ, and to give others an answer for the hope within us.

Peter's letter is a reminder for Christian pilgrims to look at their passports occasionally so we'll remember we're citizens of another kingdom, purchased by the blood of Jesus, and headed toward an inheritance that can never fade away.

KEY THOUGHT:

Suffering is an opportunity to walk
in our Lord's steps and live as pilgrims
in a pagan world.

KEY VERSES:

"Do not think it strange concerning the
fiery trial which is to try you, as though
some strange thing happened to you;
but rejoice to the extent that you
partake of Christ's sufferings."
1 Peter 4:12-13

KEY ACTION:

"Sanctify the Lord God in your hearts, and always
be ready to give a defense to everyone who asks
you a reason for the hope that is in you."
1 Peter 3:15

KEY PRAYER:

Father, allow me to see the
advantages of adversity and bring
honor to You in every circumstance.

II PETER

If you were dying but had the opportunity of writing a final letter to friends, what would you say? That's a heavy question, but it helps us understand 2 Peter. Knowing his remaining time was short, Peter wrote this letter, probably from Rome, as he neared the time of his martyrdom.

Had you been Peter, what would you have written? Perhaps you'd want to give a reminder of your core beliefs, then you might leave instructions about a critical issue, finally you'd focus on the joy of Christ's return.

That's exactly what Peter did in the three chapters of his letter. In chapter 1, he affirmed that God has given us all things pertaining to life and godliness, and we must diligently grow in these virtues. He said, "I think it is right, as long as I am in this tent (of my body) to stir you up by reminding you" (2 Peter 1:14) of the truths of Scripture given by those "who spoke as they were moved by the Holy Spirit" (2 Peter 1:21).

In chapter 2, he warned us against false teachers who speak with great swelling words of emptiness.

He concluded with chapter 3 devoted to the Lord's return, when the heavens will pass away with a great noise and the elements will melt with fervent heat. In light of this what sort of people ought we to be? We should be people who are known, Peter said, by our holy conduct and godliness, as we look for and hasten the coming of our Lord.

KEY THOUGHT:

While awaiting our Lord's return,
we must stand on His great and
precious promises, which provide
all we need for life and godliness.

KEY VERSE:

"Therefore, brethren, be even more diligent to make your call and election sure, for if you do these things you will never stumble."
2 Peter 1:10

KEY ACTION:

"Therefore, beloved, looking forward to these things, be diligent to be found by Him in peace, without spot and blameless."
2 Peter 3:14

KEY PRAYER:

Dear God, may I grow in the grace and knowledge of my Lord and Savior, Jesus Christ.

I JOHN

In a world of complexity, people crave simplicity. Retailers use simple slogans to sell us products, and the best teachers make complicated issues as simple as ABC. Steve Jobs, cofounder of Apple Computers, said, "Simple can be harder than complex. You have to work hard to get your thinking clean, to make it simple. But it's worth it in the end because once you get there you can move mountains."

That describes 1 John. It's deep as the ocean, yet simple enough for anyone to read with benefit. John didn't write in a linear way, so his book is hard to outline. But its circular style corresponds to the way we live and learn. John emphasized a number of subjects—love, light, knowledge, life—and kept circling back to them throughout his letter. He presents Jesus as the Son of God who came in flesh. Those who reject Him are heretics, antichrists, and liars. Those who receive Him are children of light with assurance of everlasting life. It's as simple as that, and as certain.

The purpose of 1 John is stated at the end of the letter: "These things I have written to you who believe in the name of the Son of God that you may *know* you have eternal life" (1 John 5:13).

Christian living isn't easy, but it *is* simple and certain—a matter of staying in the light, walking with Jesus, confessing sins, loving others, and knowing we have eternal life. That's the wonderful message of 1 John.

KEY THOUGHT:

Jesus Christ is the Word made flesh.
Those who reject Him have the spirit
of antichrist. Those who receive Him
are children of light with the assurance
of everlasting life.

KEY VERSE:

"These things I have written to you
who believe in the name of the Son
of God, that you may know that
you have eternal life."
1 John 5:13

KEY ACTION:

He laid down His life for us, and we also
ought to lay down our lives for the brethren
(see 1 John 3:16).

KEY PRAYER:

Thank you, Lord, for the promise that
if I confess my sins, You are faithful
and just to forgive me of my sins and
cleanse me from all unrighteousness.

II JOHN

A strange thing has happened to the concept of "tolerance." It once meant we accepted the fact other people had a right to their own views, even if those views were different from ours, and even if they were wrong. But culture now defines tolerance as accepting all other views as being equally valid to our own.

The Bible proclaims an objective truth and an exclusive Gospel. As a result, Christians are sometimes accused of being unloving and intolerant. The message of 2 John is: We should love one other deeply, but we cannot tolerate error and evil in our homes or churches.

John addressed this short note to a woman and her children, which metaphorically may indicate a church and its members. He reminded them of the command, both old and new, to love one another. But in plain language he also warned his readers to reject the false teachers who were traveling about. Anyone who doesn't acknowledge Christ as coming in the flesh, John said, is a deceiver and an antichrist. We mustn't accept such people, he wrote, for "anyone who welcomes them shares in their wicked work" (2 John 1:11, NIV).

What a vital balance! We're to be loving, but discerning. Every day we come face-to-face with a world God loves; but we also daily encounter a world in which we must stand for the truth. Only John could have articulated such a delicate balance, and only 2 John explains it so concisely and plainly.

KEY THOUGHT:

While we must love one another
deeply, we cannot tolerate error
and evil in our churches.

KEY VERSE:

"Whoever transgresses and does not abide
in the doctrine of Christ does not have God.
He who abides in the doctrine of Christ has
both the Father and the Son."
2 John 1:9

KEY ACTION:

If we're vigilant against deceivers and deception,
we will receive a full reward without losing
the things we've worked for
(see 2 John 1:8).

KEY PRAYER:

Lord, help me to have a discerning mind
and a loving heart.

III JOHN

Dr. A. W. Tozer pointed out that a hundred pianos all tuned to the same fork will automatically be tuned to each other. In the same way when each of God's workers is tuned to Christ, we'll be in harmony with one another. But beware the discordant note. One of the joys of being a pastor, as I've been for many years, is watching how harmoniously God's people labor side-by-side for His kingdom. One of my sorrows is seeing how one person with a personal agenda, jealous spirit, or harsh personality can disrupt the work.

The apostle John faced the same thing as he wrote 3 John. He expressed gratitude for those working alongside his friend Gaius, and he encouraged them to show continued hospitality toward traveling workers. But John expressed dismay at one man, Diotrephes, who loved attention, sowed discord, and turned away John's emissaries.

This short letter, small enough to be written on a single

parchment, tells us that those who selflessly support the Lord's work are to be commended, but those serving Satan's agenda, particularly if they infiltrate the church, must be confronted.

God wants you to be a Gaius, not a Diotrephes. Maybe He doesn't intend for you to preach before an entire congregation, but He wants you to support those who do. We each have a place in God's work; and as we labor in harmony and mutual support, we're walking in truth—and that brings joy to the whole church.

KEY THOUGHT:

Those who selflessly support the Lord's cause are to be commended; those who don't must be confronted.

KEY VERSES:

"I rejoiced greatly when brethren came and testified of the truth that is in you, just as you walk in the truth. I have no greater joy than to hear that my children walk in truth."
3 John 1:3-4

KEY ACTION:

Diligently encourage God's work and show hospitality to His workers.

KEY PRAYER:

Lord, may I be faithful in the work of the Lord, encouraging the Body of Christ.

JUDE

A recent book about backpacking in Canada warns us to purchase accurate maps before hiking in remote areas. Several travelers have died by following hastily printed maps with erroneous data. Doctrine is the roadmap of life, and the New Testament writers vigorously warned against following faulty teachers. The tragedy of such heresy is the theme of the small book of Jude.

Jude grew up in the carpenter's family of Joseph and Mary. He was the half-brother of the Lord Jesus. He became a leader in the early church and apparently wanted to write a book about what he called "our common salvation." But the spread of false doctrine caused him to change subject matter and appeal to God's people to stay alert, to contend for the truth, and to keep themselves spiritually and theologically strong.

This brief letter divides into three parts. The first section exhorts God's people to contend for the faith. The second section warns against destructive teachers. The final part urges us to stand firm in truth and love. According to Jude, we're to explain and defend the Gospel as best we can while humbly rooted in the knowledge, love, and practice of the truth.

In today's world, heresy spreads with the click of a button or the turn of a knob. We must follow Jude's call to be built up in the faith of our Lord Jesus Christ and to contend earnestly for the integrity of the faith entrusted to the saints.

KEY THOUGHT:

God's people must defend the doctrines of
the faith by preserving biblical truth, battling heresy,
and humbly standing up for the Good News.

KEY VERSES:

"But you, beloved, building yourselves up on
your most holy faith, praying in the Holy Spirit,
keep yourselves in the love of God, looking for the
mercy of our Lord Jesus Christ unto eternal life."
Jude 1:20-21

KEY ACTION:

"Contend earnestly for the faith which was
once for all delivered to the saints."
Jude 1:3

KEY PRAYER:

Lord, protect me and empower me
to stand firm in truth and love.

Revelation

Business and management writer Peter Drucker said, "Trying to predict the future is like trying to drive down a country road at night with no lights while looking out the back window." None of us knows what tomorrow holds, but the Lord Jesus Christ—Alpha and Omega—knows the end from the beginning, and in the book of Revelation He tells us how history will conclude. It's true that Revelation is full of apocalyptic visions, but the very title of the book implies God wants to *reveal* His plans to us. A special blessing is promised to those who study this book, and without it our lives—as well as the Bible itself—would be incomplete.

The apostle John received Revelation while exiled on the island of Patmos. The immediate recipients were seven churches in Asia Minor.

After an opening introduction in chapter 1, and exhortations to the seven churches in chapters 2 and 3, the writer launched into chapter after chapter of vivid descriptions of the events of the Great Tribulation, leading to the dramatic moment of Christ's return in chapter 19 and a tour of our eternal home at the end of the book.

The book of Revelation tells us that regardless of what happens in life—no matter how depressing the news or difficult the times—life in Christ has a happy ending for those whose names are written in the Lamb's Book of Life, who pray: Even so, come, Lord Jesus.

KEY THOUGHT:

God has a plan for the future and for eternity. Regardless of what happens in life—no matter how depressing or difficult the news—life in Christ has a happy ending for those whose names are written in the Lamb's Book of Life.

KEY VERSE:

"And there shall be no more curse,
but the throne of God and of the Lamb shall
be in it, and His servants shall serve Him."
Revelation 22:3

KEY ACTION:

"And the Spirit and the bride say, 'Come!' And let him
who hears say, 'Come!' And let him who thirsts come.
Whoever desires, let him take the water of life freely."
Revelation 22:17

KEY PRAYER:

Even so, come, Lord Jesus!

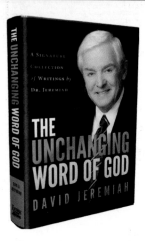

The Unchanging Word of God

Since 1982, *Turning Point* has proclaimed God's unchanging Word through the teaching ministry of Dr. David Jeremiah. You've heard him in person or over the air, through his books and his broadcasts. Dr. Jeremiah has chosen twenty popular chapters from his best-selling books and compiled them in a single volume, the distillation of three decades of ministry in pulpit and print. Topics include prayer, adversity, angels, marriage, prophecy, and more. *The Unchanging Word of God* is a treasure-trove of teaching that will inspire you to face the future with confidence and to rejoice in God's unchanging Word.

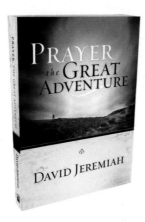

Prayer—the Great Adventure

We all need wisdom for the journey of faith that we are on, and there is no greater outlet for the Christian than going to God in prayer, seeking His wisdom for our daily lives. In this book by Dr. Jeremiah, you will learn the roadmap for prayer, and how it will affect your praise, priorities, provision, personal relationships, and protection. Learn why we can't be too busy to pray, and much more in *Prayer—the Great Adventure*.

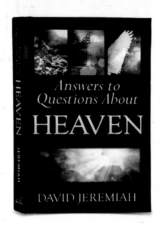

Answers to Questions About Heaven

When it comes to heaven, you have questions; the Bible has answers. Based on a lifetime of studying the biblical doctrine of heaven, Dr. David Jeremiah provides answers to questions about our heavenly destination in this informative, easy-to-read book. *Answers to Questions About Heaven* will whet your appetite for the place Jesus is preparing for us and will leave you offering afresh the last prayer of the Bible: "Even so, come, Lord Jesus!"